y

YORK FILM NOTES

The Battleship Potemkin

Director
Sergei Eisenstein

Note by Keith Withall

Longman

y York Press

York Press
322 Old Brompton Road, London SW5 9JH

Pearson Education Limited
Edinburgh Gate, Harlow, Essex CM20 2JE, United Kingdom
Associated companies, branches and representatives throughout
the world

First published 2000

ISBN 0-582-40490-8

Designed by Vicki Pacey
Phototypeset by Gem Graphics, Trenance, Mawgan Porth, Cornwall
Colour reproduction and film output by Spectrum Colour
Printed in Malaysia, KVP

contents

acknowledgements

The author is indebted to:

Ian Christie of Birkbeck College, University of London for talking to me about Eisenstein's films and the various prints of these.

Bob Geogeghan of the Archive Film Agency who advised me about early cinema.

Thank you also to Andrew Youdell, Jim Riley, Briony Dickson and the Reading Room staff at the British Film Institute.

author of this note The earliest film the author remembers seeing is *Bambi*. He saw *Potemkin* in the early 1960s as well as political films from Cuba, China and the New Waves. He is currently a freelance writer and lecturer on film and media, and has published articles in *Race and Class*, *In the Picture*, *Film Education* and *Film Dope*

background

Sitting down to watch *The Battleship Potemkin* is like setting out to see one of those other great works of art, famous but often unseen. Michelangelo's Sistine Chapel frescoes would be a good example – we may have seen the famous figure of god breathing life into Adam behind the credits of the Hollywood film – but we probably have little idea of the overall composition of the piece. Craning your neck and vision upwards to the ceiling in the actual chapel is rather different from a glossy reprint on a slide or in a book.

Potemkin is similar, so many of us have watched the six or seven minutes of the Odessa Steps Sequence, and if we haven't watched it, we are as likely to have heard of it. The part has become greater than the whole. Whilst the Steps sequence forms the dramatic and visual climax of the film, it depends on the whole film for its meaning and effect. Both as a cinematic experience and as a seminal example of film-making, all five parts of *Potemkin* are important, meaningful and memorable.

trailer

When the film appeared critics were impressed not just by the power of the massacre on the Steps, but by the whole film.

> Here, at last, the true victory of Soviet cinematography; here, at last, an authentic work of contemporary Cinematographic art, deeply thrilling in its perfection.

> One must not make petty historical demands of *The Battleship Potemkin*. Perhaps the insurrection of the *Potemkin* did not take place exactly as the screen shows it.

> But what of it, when the director Eisenstein, in collaboration with

trailer background

the cameraman Tissé, has succeeded in expressing the very spirit of the revolution, its deep dynamics, its gigantic rhythm.

N. Volkov in Trud, 1 January, 1926
in Marshall ed., 1978, p. 94

Audiences were equally enthusiastic, as an accompanist recalls:

The hall had never sat so hushed and attentive. The further the picture advanced with its weighty mass, the more frequently did bursts of applause rise from the hall ... The picture's last shots and the avalanche of final chords. The whole hall, standing, applauds.

Lev Arnshtam
in Marshall ed., 1978, p. 112

The film's impact was even greater when it was distributed abroad. In Germany a critic wrote of 'An event in cinematography of such staggering significance ...' (Marshall ed., 1978, p. 123).

The German Censors also found it staggering, and paid the film the unintentional compliment of trying to ban it. In Britain the film was banned, and remained so until the 1950s. Audience responses provided ammunition for such censorship. Luis Buñuel recalled:

Among the films that made a strong impression on me was *Battleship Potemkin*, and even now I feel again the emotion it aroused in all of us. When we left the theatre, on a street near Alésia, we started erecting barricades ourselves. The police had to intervene before we would stop.

Luis Buñuel, 1984, pp. 87–8

When it reached the USA the response was the same. Even in Hollywood where a mogul proposed:

It was my privilege a few months ago to be present at two private screenings of what is unquestionably one of the greatest motion pictures ever made, *The Armoured Cruiser Potemkin*, made in Russia under the supervision of the Soviet Government.

THE BATTLESHIP POTEMKIN

'a technique entirely new to the screen'

I shall not here discuss the commercial or political aspects of the picture, but simply say that regardless of what they may be, the film is a superb piece of craftsmanship. It possesses a technique entirely new to the screen, and I therefore suggest that it might be advantageous to have the organisation view it in the same way that a group of artists might view and study a Rubens or a Raphael.

David O. Selznick, 15 October 1946
in Marshall ed., 1978, p. 189

A similar compliment was paid by Nazi Minister for Propaganda, Josef Goebbels, who suggested the film-makers of the Third Reich should make a 'German *Potemkin*'. The advice was put into practice in a 1941 film, *Ohm Krüger*, which made propaganda out of the British imperialist war against the Boers in Southern Africa. A scene set outside a concentration camp is obviously modelled on the Odessa Steps.

By this stage *Potemkin* had become a seminal work in world cinema. Influencing film-makers, providing a model for film theory and criticism, and continuing to circulate as 'one of the great films of all times'. The final accolade came in the 1950s. *Sight & Sound*, in its first poll (repeated every decade) of film-makers and directors saw *Potemkin* voted 'best film'. An international questionnaire from the Brussels National Film Library also voted *Potemkin* the 'best film of all times'. And the vote was repeated by an international jury of film critics in 1958 at the Brussels World Fair. In 1992 *Potemkin* still managed to reach the top ten in the *Sight & Sound* Critics Poll. In the centenary year of cinema, 1995, a Film Education poll of teachers listed 'ten films that shook the world'; *Potemkin* was the only silent film, the only pre-1940 film and, indeed, the only foreign language film, in the list. Despite its great age and different form from contemporary film, *The Battleship Potemkin* continues to circulate. It turns up regularly in regional film theatres, film societies and on film courses. Though on the latter, as pointed out above, it is often the famous fourth part on the Odessa Steps that is seen rather than the complete film. Hopefully this book will suggest some reasons for viewing the whole 70 minutes or so of the film.

reading potemkin

This *Note* should appear as we approach the seventy-fifth anniversary of the first screening of *Potemkin*, 21 December 1925. In the intervening years all the subjects of the film and the film-makers who recreated the story have died. The society that produced this unusual and distinctive film has collapsed. The medium in which this story is told has been transformed in both style and techniques.

cinematic background

For a 1920s' audience the film would have fitted into their overall experience of cinema. The key differences from today would have been:

■ Aspect ratio (screen shape)

The screen's shape is denoted by the term aspect ratio, which expresses the horizontal dimension in relation to the vertical dimension. Contemporary wide screens are letter-box shaped; aspect ratios vary from 1.6:1 up to 2.4:1. Silent films still followed the dimensions produced by using photographic 35mm film as cine stock, and were almost square - 1.17:1 to 1.33:1.

early film 1.33:1   modern film 1.80:1

Sergei Eisenstein, the director of *Potemkin* actually advocated a square screen. The shape obviously gave different possibilities for composition within the frame. It is also likely that audiences scanned the image vertically (the silent screen seems to be very high to a modern eye), rather than horizontally, as is usual with the modern letter-box shape.

background   cinematic

■ **Speed film passes over lens**
The speed at which film passed through the projector was different. Sound film, using electrically powered motors, runs at 24fps (frames per second, that is, the number of frames which pass over the lens each second). In the 1920s, silent film theatres usually had motorised projectors, but many films were still recorded on machines cranked by hand. The pioneer film-makers, also hand-cranking, had run the film as slow as 14fps, just fast enough for the human eye and brain to perceive motion in a series of still images.

David Mayer (Mayer, 1972), in a shot-by-shot breakdown of the print from the Museum of Modern Art, suggests 16fps for *Potemkin*. In this version the famous three stone lions which unexpectedly appear at the end of the Odessa Steps' sequence cover 41 frames – which the audience sees for not quite three seconds. However, more recent screenings have used 20-24fps, speeds common towards the end of the silent period. Now the three lions pass over the screen in less than two seconds: in the third second the audience now sees the gates of the headquarters of the generals.

The modern technique of step-printing, or 'stretched prints', adds a further complication. In this process, frames are added to accomodate the often faster sound speeds. An extra frame is added for every existing two. Now the stone lions cover 58 frames and the audience sees them for two and a third seconds.

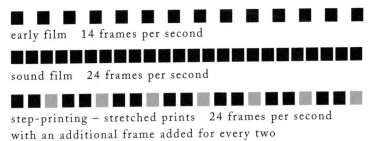

early film   14 frames per second

sound film   24 frames per second

step-printing – stretched prints   24 frames per second
with an additional frame added for every two

The discrepancies are small, but they affect the images, and possibly audience response (see Style, Director's cut, and Context, Audience). Over the whole film such changes become more significant. Video in the UK runs at 25fps, one frame faster than film, but over 100 minutes of film the video

cinematic background

version is four minutes shorter. A change of projector can alter the running time of Potemkin from 78 minutes to 58 minutes. Step-printing may add 4-5,000 extra frames to the film.

■ Intertitles (title cards)

The most dramatic difference is the absence of synchronised sound. The use of title cards – intertitles – provided techniques for giving written information to the audience. Some of this information was about plot or a commentary upon it, some dialogue which the characters spoke. The title cards could be easily translated into other languages, facilitating circulation. They were also often decorated and artistic images in their own right.

> Revolution is the only
> lawful, equal, effectual war.
> It was in Russia that
> this war was declared
> and begun. LENIN

comment

> "We, the sailors
> of the Potemkin, must stand
> in the first lines of the
> revolution with our brothers,
> the workers."

The Off Duty Watch

dialogue   plot

■ Film stock

The film stock gave black and white images. It was nitrate stock, and inflammable. Modern safety film, even black and white stock, has different tones and luminosity. In the mid-1920s colour film was still experimental; however, film-makers had developed a series of techniques for adding colour, including tones, dyes and hand-painting the frame. So, in some scenes, *Potemkin*'s flag was hand-painted red, and some prints today reproduce that.

■ Sound and music

Whilst synchronised sound was missing, music was usually provided. Rather than being recorded on the film and included in the projection, in silent cinema music and other effects were provided separately, most commonly by a single pianist or organist, or, for special events and in more expensive cinemas, by an orchestra. Potemkin was, in fact, provided with specially composed music played while the film was projected. This, of course, required composition and performance as carefully timed as for recorded soundtrack music.

The audience of those times would probably have been surprised to learn that seventy-five years later this film still circulated. Film then seemed as instantaneous and as ephemeral as much contemporary television.

social & political background

The newly emerged Soviet Union was still rebuilding from the First World War, from the Revolution that deposed the Tsar and the semi-feudal hierarchy that controlled Russia, and from the Civil War against Tsarist forces supported by the Imperialist powers, Britain ,France and the USA. In the aftermath, industry, including that of film, was short of skilled labour, equipment and materials.

The Civil War of 1917 had seen a series of revolutions and counter-revolutions, with the Bolsheviks, under Lenin, seizing victory and power in October. Their Communist programme of radical transformation was disrupted by the Civil War against the Whites (pro-Tsarists), and the resulting devastation of cities, countryside and productive forces. Despite their policy of abolishing commodity production and a market economy, 1920 saw a New Economic Policy (NEP) which allowed the buying and selling of goods for profit by private enterprise. This prompted an upturn in economic activity.

social & political background

Film Distribution recommenced and film theatres reopened. The antagonism for Bolshevism in the West, plus the Soviet Union's economic problems, meant that the supply of films from abroad, including Hollywood, was slow to develop, though there were always some western mainstream films (mostly pre-war prints) circulating. Home production was minuscule, most of the existing film-makers had decamped with the aristocracy and the capitalists. Little equipment remained in working order and film stock was like gold dust. Gradually a new cinema emerged (see Contexts).

Constructivist publicity for the film

A fever of production and experimentation was to be found in culture and the arts, including cinema. The revolutionary culture of 1920s' Soviet Russia encouraged *avant-garde* practice in every sphere of culture. In art, constructivists manipulated machine-like images, some of them providing the striking posters that publicised the films. In the theatre, poets and playwrights like Mayakovsky were active, and took a keen interest in cinema. And the young composer Dmitri Shostakovich, who composed several film scores, eked out his livelihood by accompanying silent films on the piano. They were heady times, the establishment and the hierarchy had vanished: there was little to rein in youthful enthusiasm. Young adventurous film-makers included not only Sergei Eisenstein, but Dziga Vertov and Vsesolod Pudovkin, whom we shall meet again (see Narrative, and Contexts).

Epic works were also common in this period. Red power ushered in a red calendar of important events and anniversaries.

By 1920 it contained: Bloody Sunday (9 January, the day of the 1905 execution [when troops fired on a peaceful demonstration, led by a priest, outside the Winter Palace]), Liebknecht and Luxemburg Memorial Day (17 January [they were the executed leaders of the failed German Revolution of 1919]), Woman Worker Day (8 March), Commemoration of the Paris Commune (18 March), The Arrival of Lenin in Petrograd (16 April [this was the renamed St Petersburg]), July Events (3–16 July [a massacre of a workers' demonstration, depicted in October]), Memorial Day of Moscow Armed Uprising (22 December) and, of course, Mayday, Red Army Day, and the Anniversary of the Great October Socialist Revolution.

Yuri Tsivian, 1996, p. 15

The article also describes some of the mass pageants, such as a reenactment of the storming of the winter palace in 1920, which fed into the revolutionary films, like a later film by Eisenstein, *October*.

Nineteen twenty-five was the anniversary year of the failed revolution of 1905. Then had been seen the previously most widespread and determined rebellion against the autocracy. For the young Soviet Union 1905 was an important precedent, an earlier inspiration and a set of lessons from the past. An anniversary film was commissioned, initially to be titled *1905*. Its outline sketched a panorama of six episodes covering events from the whole year and from many different parts of Russia.

1 Russo-Japanese War

2 January 9 (Bloody Sunday) and the following wave of strikes

3 Peasant Risings

social & political background

4 General Strike and its liquidation
5 Reaction attacks – Jewish pogroms, Armenian massacres
6 Krasnaya Presnaya (fresh red/beauty)

The Russo-Japanese war started in 1904. 1905 was a year of successive Russian defeats, including a major naval disaster. This defeat to Russian military, economic and imperial status sent shock waves through an antiquated and autocratic structure. It also coincided with growing radical and revolutionary movements for democratic change. The actual spark was provided in early January when the Tsar's guards killed over 100 members of a peaceful demonstration outside St Petersburg's Winter Palace (Bloody Sunday). This repressive measure sparked off a wave of strikes, riots and violent rebellions.

There followed a year-long conflict. There were violent upsurges by workers and peasants, the intelligentsia, and religious leaders. In response Tsar Nicholas II vacillated between repression and conciliation. Late in the year he conceded representative government and basic civil liberties, embodied in the Manifesto of 30 October. (Dates are in the pre-Revolutionary calendar, add ten days for the equivalent date in modern western calendar – thus the anniversary of the October Revolution is now in November.) However, in the following years, as the Tsar backtracked on his promises and the First World War again battered the fragile Russian state, popular sentiment moved progressively towards the radical wing. Thus 1917, in a sense, was a rerun of 1905 with a revolutionary closure that proved tragic for the Tsar and his family.

This epic canvas proved rather too grand for fulfilment. By the time the commission actually came to filming, the plot focused on one famous event, a mutiny on a Russian battleship. The following events occurred over eleven days in late June. *Potemkin* was part of the Russian Black Sea fleet, its sailors refused to eat maggoty meat. The attempted repression by officers sparked off a mutiny, led by Social Revolutionaries, including Seaman Afanasy Matushenko. During the mutiny, a seaman was killed and most of the officers. Having seized the ship, and the accompanying torpedo boat N267, the mutineers sailed into the harbour of Odessa, The city was already in a ferment, with strikes, attempted suppression by the

the borsch was bad

army and simmering rebellion. The ship's mutineers became a focus of popular resentment. The corpse of a dead sailor was placed on the quay with a notice:

> Before you lies the body of Gregori Vakulinchuk, a sailor killed by the senior officer of the battleship *Kniaz Potemkin* for complaining the borsch was bad. Let us make the sign of the cross and say, 'Peace to his ashes.' Let us avenge ourselves on our oppressors. Death to Them! And hurrah for freedom.
>
> Richard Hough, 1960, p. 68

The bier became a rallying point for the dissident elements in the city, Whilst the authorities debated how to regain control, the *Potemkin* mutineers threatened to bombard the city with their 12in guns. General Kokhanov, commanding, sent Cossacks to clear the quayside. Accounts differ, but rioting, looting and arson were taking place. During the night troops fired on crowds on the Richelieu Steps and around the harbour. Hundreds were killed, some by gunfire, others in burning warehouses. The guns of *Potemkin* did not open fire, the sailors were unaware of events on shore and were also caught up in arguments about what course of action to follow. When relative calm was imposed on the city the sailors organised the funeral of Vakulinchuk. Some sort of fracas developed and sailors were killed. After this the *Potemkin* did open fire on the city, but found it impossible to target the military accurately. Then came news that the Russian Black Sea fleet was approaching. When Potemkin sailed for their first encounter a supporting mutiny broke out on battleship *George the Conqueror* (*Georgy Pobyedonosets*). The two ships returned triumphantly to Odessa. Divisions amongst the crew of the *George* led to an abortive sailing, the sailors surrendering to the authorities. This event undermined the confidence of the *Potemkin* mutineers. They left Odessa and avoiding the searching Russian fleet, found refuge at Constanza in Romania. The Russian government recovered the *Potemkin* and it court-martialled those of the mutineers it could lay hands on; most received sentences of penal servitude. Matushenko came back in 1907 under amnesty, but was then tried and hanged. Many of the mutineers emigrated, elsewhere in Europe or even to the Americas. This brief episode provided an example of both rebellion and repression which were the main memories of 1905.

key players' biographies

The Commission for scripting the anniversary film had been given to Nina Agadzhanova-Shutko. She had been involved in the Bolshevik underground organisation, known as 'old Bolsheviks'. She worked as a scriptwriter for a number of films, including works by Kuleshov and Pudovkin (see Contexts). Whilst she was working on the original epic conception, a young first-time film-maker attracted attention with a film about worker's rebellion and capitalist suppression – *Strike*. This was Sergei Eisenstein, who was assigned to direct the proposed *1905* film. Eisenstein recalls Nina Agadzhanova-Shutko:

> [She] was the one human being who extended a helping hand to me at a very critical period of my creative life ... she instilled in me a true sense of the historical revolutionary past.
>
> Richard Taylor ed., 1995, pp. 148, 150

However, whilst her preparatory work was important in the gestation of the film, it is clear that the actual (constantly changing) shooting script was mainly Eisenstein's. It was Eisenstein who decided that the sequence (originally 42 shots) about a shipboard mutiny and harbour massacre should become the entire film: an episode that represented the larger events of 1905.

Born into a bourgeois family, Eisenstein had been recruited into the Red Army as a student during the Civil War. He became involved in theatre and propaganda and his gifts for design and caricature became quickly apparent. When demobilised he opted out of his engineering studies and soon ended up in the new, revolutionary theatre. Here he met and worked with some of the outstanding artists in the new world of Soviet Art (see Contexts).

Eisenstein was notable for his liking for effects, circus-style exhibition and an increasing demand for realism. This was demonstrated in his production of *The Mexican*, a story by Jack London, set around the Mexican revolution of 1910.

> In the interlude between Acts One and Two, fairylights lit up the proscenium arch and the revolutionary leaders came forward to harangue the audience about the evils of capitalism, especially as manifested in Mexico. The speech ended with a policeman arresting the speaker as an agitator. Two clowns rushed out and knocked the policeman down. [Then] Eisenstein ... placed a boxing ring downstage, as close to the audience as possible, with 'real fighting bodies crashing to the ring floor, panting, the shine of sweat on torsos, and finally, the unforgettable smacking of gloves against taut skin and strained muscles.
>
> Ronald Bergan, 1997, p. 71

His last major theatrical piece was a play *Gas Masks*, performed in an actual gas works between shifts.

> *Gas Masks* with its general aims ... was the last possible attempt within the confines of theatre to overcome its sense of illusion ... in fact that was already almost cinema, which builds its effects on precisely that kind of theatrical 'material' through montage juxtaposition ... The theatre had become too confined for his imagination. As he explained, 'the cart dropped to pieces, and its driver dropped into the cinema.'
>
> Ronald Bergan, 1997, p. 83

His first feature film, *Strike*, released in 1925, exemplified experimentation and eclecticism. It was produced by the Proletkult collective, based at the Central Moscow Theatre. It had been intended to produce an epic seven-part series of films on *Towards the Dictatorship of the Proletariat*. This ambitious plan was limited by the resources available in Soviet Cinema. *Strike* was the only episode to be filmed. It is divided into six parts, a common device in Soviet Cinema for many theatres only had one projector, which meant having to stop at intervals to change the reel. Both *Strike* and *Potemkin* were structured around these successive reel changes.

Strike presages the later films in other ways: the use of powerful editing or montage, casting in terms of typage or types, caricature (see Style and

Contexts). It also includes both eccentric and circus-style sequences which are less apparent in the later films. In this way it was typical of the youthful exploration and enthusiasm of Soviet art. Cinema was to prove the ideal medium for this approach. And Eisenstein became the most noted exponent of the new cinema, developing innovative techniques in a series of powerful dramas.

■ *Strike*, 1924 – uses montage, but also eccentric acting and staging

■ *Potemkin*, 1925 – uses montage within a more disciplined narrative structure

■ *October*, 1928 – deals with the actual revolution of 1917, uses montage in a more strictly intellectual way

■ *The Old and the New*, 1929 – deals with the collectivisation of agriculture; develops overtonal montage (see Style for more on montage)

His career in the 1930s and the new sound cinema was to be much more erratic. In 1930 he (with two colleagues Alexandrov and Tissé) visited first Europe and then the USA. He planned to make a film in Hollywood, an idealistic notion. He did begin making a film in Mexico, funded by Upton Sinclair. When Sinclair withdrew his financial support, Eisenstein and his companions were forced to return home, and he was never able to finish the Mexican film, *Que Viva Mexico*.

In the Soviet Union in the 1930s Revolutionary Socialist Construction had degenerated into Revolutionary Isolationism. Soviet interests took precedence over International Proletarian interests. Culturally, revolutionary vanguardism was to be stifled by Socialist Realism. Making films that appeared difficult or ambiguous was formalism (see Contexts).

A prime example of formalism was Eisenstein's use of montage, especially in *October*. He made a number of films under the new prescription, but his work was always troubled. He also taught at the Soviet Film school, and wrote extensively.

■ *Bezhin Meadow* – was to tell the story of a young socialist hero, killed by his father in a dispute over collectivisation. This was suppressed, and only fragments remain

■ *Alexander Nevsky* – Nevsky was a Russian prince who led the defeat of the invading Teutonic Knights in the thirteenth century. It was a success, partly due to it providing a metaphor for the Soviet Communism–German Fascism antagonism. Even so, several sequences, possibly an entire reel were cut

■ *Ivan the Terrible Parts 1 and 2* – Ivan was regarded as the unifier of Russia in the sixteenth century. Part 1 was successful, providing parallels with the struggle against the German invasion; Part 2 ran into problems of formalism and parallels with events and characters much closer to home. Part 2 is now seen as a cinematic and historical metaphor for what is called Stalinism. In 1946 it was banned and the proposed Part 3 was never completed

This was his last film, Eisenstein died in 1949.

For *Potemkin* Eisenstein was able to use a group of assistants who had worked previously on *Strike*, and a number of whom were to become long-time film companions.

Eduard Tissé was director of photography on all Eisenstein's films. He was born in Lithuania in 1897. During the Civil War he was employed as a newsreel cameraman. He worked with Eisenstein from *Strike* onwards. His cinematography for Eisenstein is distinctive and a powerful contribution to the film's style. Tissé was also inventive in terms of camera technology: the filming of the Odessa Steps sequence being a prime example. None of his work with other directors has achieved the status of his cinematography with Eisenstein.

There were Eisenstein's 'iron five': Grigori Alexandrov, Maxim Strauch, Mikhail Gomorov, Alexander Antonov, Alexander Leyshin – actors who had left the Proletcult theatre with him in 1924.

> We were actor-students of the First Workers' Theatre of the Proletcult and played in all Eisenstein's productions and in his first film, *Strike*. Besides this, we performed subsidiary jobs in the theatre: Alexandrov was in charge of props; Antonov was a

key players background

fitter, responsible for erecting supports for the tightropes along which Alexandrov and Golutvin walked; I had to do most of the painting chores. We didn't shun any kind of work and did everything happily, cheerfully and enthusiastically. Such a principle and style of work, without division into 'artists' and 'artisans', proved to be an excellent school for us, the future assistant – 'Potemkinists'.

A. Levshin
in Marshall ed., 1978, p. 65

Alexandrov was the key member of this little group. He worked on all Eisenstein's silent films, usually as assistant director, and was often responsible for second location work. He also accompanied Eisenstein and Tissé on their trip to the west. Later on he compiled a feature-length version of Eisenstein's Mexican footage, *Que Viva Mexico*. Ivor Montagu, who wrote a book about Eisenstein in Hollywood, describes Alexandrov as 'slim, strong, handsome, fair-haired and golden-skinned athlete – an Adonis' (Bergan, 1997, p. 72).

Eisenstein's sexual biography is vague and ambiguous, but he had definite gay predilections. This may partly explain his close relationship with Alexandrov, though Montagu added that there was no actual sexual relationship and that Alexandrov was definitely heterosexual. In the sound era Alexandrov became a director in his own right, being a pioneer in the socialist realist musical.

There is little information available in English on Edmund Meisel, who composed the accompanying score for the film. The following is a summary of an extended biography and appreciation in German: 'Born 14 August 1894 in Vienna; 1910 family moved to Berlin; 1912–14 violinist in the Berlin Bluethner and Philharmonic Orchestra; 1918–26 worked as conductor, worked in theatre and film as composer; 1924 married Els Peters; 1930–33 moved to England; 1944 died in London aged 40.

'From 1924 onwards Meisel worked in the theatre; having to make a choice, he broke with classical concert music and decided to work with Piscator in his experimental theatre. Piscator's theatre operated as a collective – for example, the script was sometimes written after the scene

the possibilities of music in film

was arranged – and music was an integral part of the collective work. Meisel was politically left wing although this was due more to a sympathy of ideas than political conviction. His ideas were to draw a theoretical differentiation between bourgeois and class-aware left-wing music. From 1927 to 1928 Meisel composed his best known music for films: *The Battleship Potemkin* (1926), *Berlin City Symphony* (1927) and *October* (1928).

'Film music was usually put together from pieces by different composers, according to the mood of the scene, and because of the cost very rarely was new music composed. The orchestra leader was employed by the cinema-owner and the music was put together between production and distribution – usually in two or three days. In provincial cinemas the musicians would play during the screening, as they saw the film for the first time. Meisel composed his own scores and worked closely with Walter Ruttman (for *Berlin City Symphony*) and Eisenstein.

'Meisel's fame spread with *Potemkin*. His compositions awakened discussion about film music and entered into everyone's consciousness on a level never experienced before. The film industry became impressed by the possibilities of music in film, directly as a result of *Potemkin*. Meisel himself profited from this fame and was invited to play at home and abroad' (Sudendorf, 1989).

For all these members of the production team *Potemkin* remains their most famous film.

director as auteur

Auteurisme became a key concept in film study when the young French critics and film-makers of the New Wave began to treat Hollywood films as art. Their key tactic was to elevate the director as the 'author' of style and meaning in an artistic film. In this sense there can be no doubt that Eisenstein qualifies as an auteur, one of the most significant in cinema history. It is clear from both Eisenstein's writings and from those of his colleagues that he was the key and dominant creative force in *Potemkin*, and all his other films. He was responsible for the script, as well as direction, and personally edited the film. This mastery of an artistic

director as auteur

the relationship between form and meaning

medium was already apparent before he moved to cinema – in his stage work.

As we have seen, he made only seven feature films (and several short, and incomplete ones), but each is an important film in terms of world cinema. *Potemkin* is probably the most famous, and *October* and *The Old and the New* are key films in the silent *oeuvre* –influential in form and style. *Alexander Nevsky* is a key film in terms of the integration of music into a film. And the surviving two parts of *Ivan the Terrible* are not just monuments to the repression under Stalin, but key texts, notably in the use of colour in the second part.

The style of *Potemkin* is examined in Style, but a reader can also pursue this analysis across Eisenstein's other films. Such a study would demonstrate how, not just in editing, but in other ways, we can see continuities and developments. (David Bordwell, 1993, is an excellent source for this.)

As well as his films Eisenstein left a large legacy of theoretical writing on cinema and art in a more general sense. There one will find very full discussions about the relationship between form and meaning in his films. The care and attention he lavished to achieve specific meanings in these films are also apparent in them. The body of writing (still not completely available in English) is one of the most important sources of film theory. Eisenstein discusses storytelling, cinematic techniques, audiences and their responses, and the political content he considers necessary in a revolutionary cinema (see Style and Contexts for more on Eisenstein's theoretical contribution). Unlike the majority of film directors, Eisenstein has provided the most persuasive analysis of his own work.

narrative & form

film narrative

CAUSE AND EFFECT:
LINEAR AND NONLINEAR STRUCTURES

Potemkin, like all Eisenstein's films, offers the audience a story. Narrative is the dominant form of cinema, offering a clearly laid-out sequence of interconnected events, usually on a cause-effect basis. Not all film-makers in the 1920s' Soviet Union considered narrative a suitable form for revolutionary politics. The most extreme example would be Dziga Vertov, who regularly railed against the tyranny of narrative cinema. His most famous film, *Man with a Movie Camera*, exemplifies this. It presents a picture of Moscow through twenty-four hours, but what organises the film are not the developments through the day, but a series of themes that illustrate both the city and socialist culture.

At the opposite extreme would be Pudovkin. His film of Gorky's novel, *Mother*, was also part of the 1905 commemoration. It has distinctive editing, and is full of revolutionary fervour; however, the narrative is instantly recognisable to spectators accustomed to the Hollywood model. The story centres on a young worker and his mother; the chain of events that befall them have a strict linear development and follow a cause-effect sequence. Whilst the ending is tragic, it offers a clear resolution. Horrified by the death of her son, the mother dies upholding the red flag against the charging military. Thus it offers the audience both red politics and mainstream film closure: a resolution that ends the story and enables the audience to 'put it down'.

Eisenstein's films fall between the two extremes: they all have an overall story structure and have some sort of resolution. But, some, like *Strike*, have more in common with Bertolt Brecht's epic drama than the mainstream. Brecht, a revolutionary playwright working from the 1920s onwards, advocated creating a 'distance' between the drama and the audience. One aspect of the strategy for achieving this was a story structure that lent itself to varying orders; another was to insert 'voices' from outside the story.

In *Strike*, the episodic structure of the plot breaks down the continuity found in more linear drama. *October* is also less than straightforward: the first half of the film subordinates narrative development to political exploration and imagery, whilst the latter half is more linear. Both these films include material that is not part of the world of the story, not within the diegesis: that is, Eisenstein includes visual symbols that a spectator will not recognise from the already supplied information in the plot. In *Strike* this is the cutting-in of images of the slaughtering of a bull as mounted troops charge the workers: in *October* a series of figures of deities, as a reactionary general leads an attack on the Provisional Government. Both rely on the audience making intellectual connections and then 'reading' the image.

Potemkin offers the clearest example of a direct narrative in Eisenstein's silent films. (*Alexander Nevsky* would be the equivalent amongst the sound films.) The basic plot follows the events on the battleship, and the mutiny. We move to Odessa, see the popular demonstrations, followed by the massacre on the Steps. And then the *Potemkin* sails towards the Squadron and the support of those sailors provides an upbeat ending to the film story. This clear chain of events is presented chronologically, and avoids flashbacks. The development of the story clearly depicts cause and effect, the actions are motivated – even a spectral image is motivated: 'Before the eyes of one old sailor, there begins to swim ... the vision of the sailors hanging on the yard-arm' (Sergei Eisenstein, 1968, p. 44). We shall return to disruptions within the narrative at the end of this part.

narration in potemkin

The film is clearly designed so that the audience's perceptions are positioned with the sailors and ordinary people. Thus *Potemkin* offers a generally restricted narration. The most commanding narrative for audience is omniscient. For example, in *Mother*, the spectator sees the son in prison; sees what is happening unbeknownst to him among his proletarian comrades; activity by his mother; and, separate again, the machinations of the police. In *Potemkin* we are denied this godlike view. It is true that we will know more than a particular group of characters; for example, we see Gilyarovsky in the canteen when the sailors do not, but we do not see everything. So, it is unknown how far the captain planned the execution on the quarter-deck; what the Odessa military are planning; what the commander of the admiralty squadron is planning to do. Thus, we are as surprised as the sailors when the armed marines are called; as shocked as the peaceful citizenry when the soldiers arrive; and as anxious as the sailors as the battleships draw closer and closer at the film's finale.

Like mainstream films of the time, *Potemkin* opens its narration clearly and simply. Thus, after the quotation on revolution, we immediately find ourselves on board the ship. Part I provides the audience with a sense of the setting of the action, identifies the main participants, and sets up the oppositions of the film through the conflict over maggoty meat. Its primary functions are to enable to audience to grasp both characters and settings sufficiently clearly to follow the developing plot, and to signal the ideological strands in the film. The two leading sailors are first identified for us. This is immediately followed by an example of the oppression that stirs the sailors' revolt. A little later we see the leading characters among the officers. Both our understanding and our emotions are primed for the spiralling sequence of actions that follow.

And the film provides an ending to round off the story: closure. The end of the final sequence,

> Joyfully, the sailors on the mast, in the watch-tower,
> ... on the decks
> ... and on the prow of the battleship
> ... wave their caps in the air.
> Great waves caused by the passage of the battleship.
> The tall prow of the rebellious battleship moves victoriously onwards.
>
> Sergei Eisenstein, 1968, p. 100

the audience can leave happy

Revolutionary closure –
re-interpreting history

'the laws of austere composition of tragedy'

The audience can leave happy in the positive outcome, at least for the characters with whom they have been encouraged to identify. However, the ending does not offer complete closure. The final outcome of the mutiny is not shown.

Here Eisenstein is playing with the recorded events, a fact that has generated both much discussion and much criticism. What he has actually done is not totally invent, but change the supporting mutiny on the *George the Unconquerable* to a supportive cheer of the squadron, and then just omitted the subsequent events. The commemoration required a celebratory performance, and, from the 1920s' perspective the 1905 revolution (and this mutiny) had finally had their aims achieved, by the Bolshevik-led revolution. Eisenstein's plotting of the story aims to dramatise those aspects relevant to the twenty-year commemoration. Hence also, the *Potemkin* guns fire to end the Odessa Steps massacre – not a day later as actually occurred. Keeping the plotting of the story simple and direct probably also explains why the *Torpedo Boat 267* only suddenly appears in the final meeting at sea (The 1950 sound version included an explanatory title about *267*).

chronology & temporal order

The film was conceived as a unity and is carefully structured in its plotting and in the narrative style. Eisenstein comments on and analyses this structure at length in his introduction to the screenplay:

> Outwardly, *Potemkin* is a chronicle of events but it impresses the spectators as a drama.
>
> The secret of this effect lies in the plot which is built up in accordance with the laws of austere composition of tragedy in its traditional five-act form ...
>
> This age-honoured structure of tragedy is further stressed by the subtitle each act is preceded by.

Here are the five acts:

I Men and Maggots
Exposition of the action. The conditions aboard the battleship. Meat teeming with maggots. Unrest among the sailors.

II Drama on the Quarter-Deck
'All hands on deck!' The sailors' refusal to eat the soup. The tarpaulin scene. 'Brothers!' Refusal to fire. Mutiny. Revenge on the officers.

III The Dead Man Cries for Vengeance
Mist. Vakulinchuk's body in the Odessa port. Mourning over the body. Meeting. Raising the red flag.

IV The Odessa Steps
Fraternisation of shore and battleship. Yawls with provisions. Shooting on the Odessa Steps.

V Meeting the Squadron
Night of expectation. Meeting the squadron. Engines. 'Brothers!' The squadron refuses to fire.

The action in each part is different, but the whole action is permeated and cemented, as it were, by the method of double repetition.

In 'Drama on the Quarter-Deck' a handful of mutinous sailors – part of the battleship's crew – cry '*Brothers!*' to the firing squad. The rifles are lowered. The whole of the crew joins the rebels.

In 'Meeting the Squadron' the mutinous ship – part of the navy – throws the cry '*Brothers!*' to the crews of the admiralty squadron. And the guns trained on the *Potemkin* are lowered. The whole of the fleet is at one with the *Potemkin*.

'every "transition" point ... emphasised by a pause'

From a particle of the battleship's organism to the organism as a whole; from a particle of the navy's organism – the battleship – to the navy's organism as whole. This is how the feeling of revolutionary brotherhood develops thematically; and the composition of the work on the subject of the brotherhood of workers and of revolution develops parallel with it.

Sergei Eisenstein, 1968, pp. 8–9

Eisenstein has taken the basic actions of the story and organised them thematically. He has managed to do this without altering the sequential chain of events. But he has used what is called ellipsis, the omission of certain events, to concentrate on such themes. Most noticeably, we do not see the aftermath of the mutiny: the spectator will probably infer that the officers are now all dead. A little later we do not see the aftermath of the massacre on the Steps. The response to that is strictly limited to the actions of the sailors. In both cases Eisenstein uses dramatic selection to pair down the recorded events. Most of the officers died, but three were recruited into the mutiny. And Odessa continued in a state of unrest after the ship left.

Eisenstein is also concerned to develop a structure for the audience's 'reading' of the story and its five parts:

they are perfectly *identical* in that each act is clearly divided into two almost equal parts, this division becoming more pronounced in Part II.

The tarpaulin scene – mutiny

Mourning for Vakulinchuk – meeting of indignant protest.

Fraternising – shooting.

Anxiously awaiting the squadron – triumph.

Moreover, every 'transition' point is emphasised by a pause, a *caesura*.

In Part III this is a few shots of clenched fists, showing the transition from grief for the slain comrade to infuriated protest.

In Part IV this is the title '*SUDDENLY* ...', cutting short the fraternising scene and ushering in the shooting scene.

'the motionless rifles ... the gaping mouths of the guns'

In Part II this is the motionless rifle muzzles; in Part V – the gaping mouths of the guns and the exclamation, '*Brothers!*', breaking the dead silence of expectation and arousing an avalanche of fraternal feelings.

And the remarkable thing about these dividing points is that they mark not merely a transition to a merely *different* mood, to a merely *different* rhythm, to a merely *different* event, but show each time that the transition is to a sharply opposite quality. To say that we have contrasts would not be enough: the image of the same theme is each time presented from the *opposite* point of view, although it *grows out of the theme itself.*

Thus the rebellion breaks out after the unbearable strain of waiting under the rifles (Part II).

The angry protest follows the mass mourning for the slain comrade (Part III).

The shooting on the Odessa Steps is a natural answer of the reactionaries to the fraternal embraces between the mutinous crew of the *Potemkin* and the population of Odessa (Part IV) ...

The film in its entirety is also divided near the middle by a dread halt, a *caesura*, when the tempestuous action of the first half is suspended, and the second half begins to gain impetus.

The episode with Vakulinchuk's body and the Odessa mist serves as a similar *caesura* for the film as a whole.

At that point the theme of revolution spreads from one mutinous battleship to Odessa, embracing the whole city topographically opposed to the ship but emotionally at one with it. But at the moment when the theme returns to the sea, the city is separated from it by soldiers (the episode on the steps).

Sergei Eisenstein, 1968 pp. 10–11

(Eisenstein fails to mention a caesura for Part I, but Mayer points out that such a point occurs at shot 129, an extreme close-up of a canon mouth, marking the change from agitation over the meat to the routines of the ship.)

space

Eisenstein's idea of a classical tragedy is worked out, not only in the temporal, but also in the spatial form of the film. Each of the five parts locates the action at a particular time and place. The first two acts are set on the *Potemkin*, in a single day. The following two take place in Odessa on the next day. And the final act moves through night to day and the meeting at sea.

Each locale limits the actions by the nature of its structure. Scenes on the battleship move from above to below deck, from the space of the ordinary sailors to the space of the officers. In Part I, it is the officers who move freely, thus Gilyarovsky can dominate the sailors' canteen. However, a hint of subversion, the plate smashed by the sailor, is from the officers' mess. In Part II, the events on the quarter-deck lead to the invasion of the officers' space by the sailors, notably in the fight to death in the cabin.

The different components of the image balance the composition whilst the directional flow in the image draws the spectator's eye forward with the camera

This delineation of space continues in Part III. Vakulinchuk's body established a space for the mutiny at the edge of the Odessa quay. Gradually, the growing mass of townspeople swell the space, over the wharves and up the steps. The boats to and from the battleship establish a corridor between the original mutiny and its new territory (supported by a visual motif discussed in the mise-en-scène, see Style).

The arrival of the soldiers disrupts this space with its violent massacre. The response of the *Potemkin* does not reoccupy space, but destroys it. Hence the ship returns to the original space of the mutiny, the open sea. This is both the ship's natural habitat, and also a space not controlled and hemmed in by the structure of the autocracy. It provides an alternative focus from the two spaces of the ship and the town: a contrasting ebb-and-flow motion to the regular rhythm of the battleships (see discussion of the mise-en-scène in Style and Contexts, Critical responses).

character

The oppositions that Eisenstein delineates in the narrative structure are also clearly worked out in the characterisation of the film. A series of oppositions and unities that result in the fundamental unity of the people and their opposition to Tsarism (examples of Eisenstein's casting are given in Contexts). His use of typage, people who represented a person of particular class, age, gender, enables him to use individuals, but still emphasise the group or collective. Certain individual characters stand out momentarily: Vakulinchuk on the quarter-deck, the mother on the steps; but they quickly flow back into the larger grouping. Unlike in the mainstream films, they neither determine action nor are they the focus of them. Thus reviewers frequently comment on how Potemkin dramatises the mass.

In act I the action is launched through the basic opposition between sailors and officers.

The sailors always form a collective, the opening pairing stresses a common struggle:

| the funeral bier ... a collective focus |

> The sailors Matyushenko and Vakulinchuk ...
> Matyushenko speaks urgently to Vakulinchuk:
> 'We, the sailors of Potemkin, must support the
> workers, our brothers, and must stand in the
> front ranks of the revolution.'
>
> Sergei Eisenstein, 1968, p. 27

This is followed by the sailors communally sleeping, and opposed to the individualistic NCO:

> A fat boatswain with a brutal face descends
> the ladder into the lower deck and looks with
> malice at
> ... the sleeping sailors.   p. 28

If Vakulinchuk and the young sailor are bonded to their comrades by experience and interest, this is not true of the officers, their unity is one of dominance. Even when bought together in the action, their common purpose, it is clear, results from fear or sycophancy. So when the captain raises the question of the borsch:

> Commander Golikov, one hand by the side of his
> frock-coat, the other behind his back, looks
> threateningly about him.
> A young petty officer, not knowing what to do,
> mechanically fingers the strap running over
> his shoulder.   p. 44

This theme is continued when the *Potemkin* arrives in Odessa. The funeral bier of Vakulinchuk provides a focus for the common anti-Tsarist emotions in the city. This funeral bier becomes a collective focus. Dissident elements are ejected:

The woman shouts:

> 'Mothers and brothers! Let there be no dis-
> tinctions or enemies among ourselves!'
> ... and she exhorts the crowd.
> The suspicious-looking man in the straw hat
> smiles disdainfully.

character narrative & form

```
The woman continues her speech.
The suspicious-looking man in the straw hat
cries out:
'Down with the Jews!'
... and smiles insolently.
The men standing near him
... sharply
... and angrily,
... one
... after another
... turn their heads.
The men surround and attack the reactionary.
In the Russian text he is described as
'Chyornosotyenyets': 'a member of the Black
Hundred', a virulent anti-Jewish society.    p. 67
```

The expelled man not only represents Tsarist forces, but reactionary elements that threaten the unity of the people. The Black Hundreds were involved in the anti-Jewish pogroms which were the reactionaries' response to revolution.

The wave sequence on the Steps stresses how a new collective in the city has come together in support of the sailors.

```
On the wharf, an educated young woman, an
umbrella in her hand, and a man - apparently a
professor - look ardently, but with reserve,
in the direction of the rebellious battleship.
A group of workers (two men and a woman)
tumultuously hail the rebellious sailors.
The young woman with the umbrella opens it out
joyfully and waves her black-gloved hand, and
the man with the appearance of a professor
takes off his hat.
Standing with a young schoolgirl, an elderly
woman in pince-nez rapturously waves her
hands.
A student shouts joyfully.                    p. 71
```

This joyful collective is broken up by the murderous assault of the military. The individuals singled out during the demonstration are again singled out as victims in the massacre. Eisenstein both emphasises the collective unit, but also provides individual types for the audience's identification (see discussion in Contexts, Critical responses).

In the last two parts of the film the representation of Tsarism is changed to that of a faceless enemy. We never see the faces of the troops as they descend the Steps shooting civilians. There is but the one shot of the face of the mounted Cossack, a particular image from Eisenstein's memory. In the last part, again, we never see the officers in the squadron as they and *Potemkin* steam towards each other. What we do see is the establishment of a new unity, as the ordinary sailors of the squadron join in cheering the *Potemkin* and its red flag of mutiny.

The battleship occupies a special place in the ebb and flow of oppositions in the film. Earlier reviewers commented on *Potemkin* as a character in the narrative.

> A new hero is introduced into the consciousness of the spectator. This hero is not allegorical, not stylised, not fetishistically sugary-sweet. He is real and overwhelming in his authenticity, in the power of his restored form; he is convinced by reality of his existence.
>
> This hero is the revolutionary battleship, submitting to the will of sailors' hands, sloughing off the scum of traditional privilege, the dead routine of barracks discipline, its liberated prow surging through the fresh sea.
>
> The transition-turning point from the power of admirals and captains to strong arms [of the working class], for the first time aware of their own rights and strength, is shown with staggering mastery.
>
> The whole unfamiliar setting of a warship, the power of its machinery, the peculiarity of its form, the weight of its armaments, so impresses, so intrigues the spectator's attention that one's eyes are literally riveted to the screen, for fear of missing the smallest particularity, the most minute detail of the mastery of this

character narrative & form

> mechanical monster – the structure of firmly fitted parts, with all
> its complex rigging, construction, armaments.
>
> *Nikolai Aseyev, Sovetsky Ekran, No. 1, 1926*
> in Marshall ed., 1978, pp. 248–9

The battleship expresses a particular strand of Soviet art of the period, the machine as an expression of working-class organisation and power. Machine-like images populate the Constructivist art of the period. And the film extends the machine metaphor to the actions of the film's characters. In Part I the sailors' activities on the ship are part of the way we come to know them: cleaning the ship's armaments, using its appendages in their personal actions. This metaphor expands as the film develops. A machine-like rhythm becomes more and more discernible as the film proceeds.

In Part II, the mutiny, and in particular when the sailors go to the armoury for rifles, has a particular rhythm. This rhythm reaches a crescendo on the Odessa Steps:

```
A small boy, wounded, falls nearby.
In terror the crowd runs down the steps.
The boy clutches his head with his hands.
In terror the crowd runs down the steps.
Relentless, like a machine, ranks of soldiers
with rifles trailed descend the steps.
In terror the crowd runs down the steps.
```

Sergei Eisenstein, 1968, p. 74

The guns of the battleship halt the rhythm, and a lull occurs, as after the mutiny. Then the rhythm returns, even more insistent for the final meeting.

```
The gun-turrets swing menacingly.
The gunner is prepared for battle.
The muzzles of the cannons are raised menac-
ingly.
The gunner looks at his sights.
The muzzles of the cannons are raised.
The gunner looks at his sights.
```

> The prow of the battleship cuts through the
> water,
> ... raising great waves on all sides.
>
> Sergei Eisenstein, 1968, p. 95

parallelism

Eisenstein builds a series of motifs into the narrative, both binding the story together and highlighting the themes it encompasses. His introduction to the screenplay analyses how 'Brothers!' and 'brotherhood' are patterned through the film. Naim Kleiman has noted (Introduction to BBC TV screening) how the question, 'To shoot, or not to shoot' creates a pattern in the film, from the cry of Vakulinchuk during the mutiny, to the arrival of the soldiers on the Steps, and finally to the squadron of battleships as they meet at sea. The Odessa Steps' sequence ends with the decision of the sailors to fire the guns of *Potemkin*, whereas the records show they failed to shoot at that point. However, structurally, it develops another line of opposition within the narrative.

The film's use of parallels both accentuates certain unities and oppositions within the film, the above example builds the notion of brotherhood (see Contexts, Critical responses for discussion of gender in the film). Eisenstein also builds parallels between different characters within the larger groupings. So leaders, victims and rebels are character strands in both the shipboard rebellion and the town-based rebellion. However, the final meeting at sea focuses on the brotherhood of the sailors alone.

genre

Potemkin is a melodrama of protest (Michael Walker, 1982). This is a key form in Eisenstein's work, shared by *Strike*, *Behzin Meadow* and an episode of *Que Viva Mexico*, but also a subsidiary strand in *October*, *The General Line*, *Alexander Nevsky* and *Ivan, the Terrible, Part 1*. Much of the pathos Eisenstein aimed to achieve arises from the contrasts set up by protest and repression.

merged as a powerful force in western drama and literature
jhteenth century, and examples of melodrama and the protest
)und during the French revolution – a prequel to the Russian.
By the twentieth century melodrama was one of the most popular and
potent forms of popular narrative. Built around clear oppositions and
strongly drawn characterisation, it provided an ideal format for expressing
the joys and sorrows of the newly industrialised working classes. In
particular the protest variant could give expression to the *angst* and anger
often generated by the conditions of work and life in the new capitalist
states.

Examples Eisenstein would be familiar with are the protest dramas of
D.W. Griffith. *Birth of a Nation* and *Intolerance* are both melodramas of
protest. However, they dramatise very different values:

> His tender-hearted film morals go no higher than a level of
> Christian accusation of human injustice and nowhere in his films
> is sounded a protest against social injustice.
>
> Sergei Eisenstein, 1951, p. 233–4

In a generic sense protest melodrama offers the audience a set of familiar
characters and situations, on which any individual text can play variations.
There is a tendency to offer starkly drawn and polarised characters. Thus in
Part 1 the sympathetic portrayal of the sailors contrasts with the
autocratic and arrogant officers. Eisenstein's practice of typage also lends
itself to the stark polarities of melodrama. And these polarities continue
throughout the film. In the climactic scene on the Odessa Steps the smiling
and peaceful citizenry are starkly contrasted with the brutal and faceless
soldiery of the Tsar.

A key factor in protest melodrama is the elicitation of emotional
sympathy for the oppressed through the suffering of innocents. This is
already signalled in Part II when a group of sailors is selected for execution
in an arbitrary fashion, then reinforced with the death/martyrdom
of Vakulinchuk. It becomes most powerful in Part IV when the
extended massacre on the Odessa Steps includes women, children, cripples.
This violent scene usually engenders strong indignation in the viewer

and confirms their identification with the oppressed. Hence Eisenstein's pathos.

But the protest form also requires that the cause of the oppressed shall be espoused. Thus in Part III Vakulinchuk's bier provides a focus for the solidarity felt by the citizens of Odessa. Vakulinchuk's corpse is a visible sign of the ruthless oppression visited on the innocent sailors of Potemkin.

Finally, melodramas of protest often end in defeat for the oppressed: they rarely achieve real victory. However, in order to satisfy the pathos aroused in the audience, the stories usually offer a promise of future righting of wrongs – the torch is passed on. Thus in Pudovkin's *Mother*, whilst the son and his comrades die in the police assault, the death of the mother, waving the flag of revolution, provides a visual icon. The icon leads into a final montage ending with the triumphant flag of revolution. Hence the import of Eisenstein's closing sequence. The episode of solidarity between the Black Sea Fleet and *Potemkin* not only enables the film to end on an upbeat note, it clearly tells the audience that the rebellion has been passed on to other hands. It thus provides a link with *Potemkin* and 1905 that can be seen to return in 1917.

narrative disruptions

In its use of the protest form *Potemkin* is offering an alternative to mainstream melodramas like those of Griffith, but this might seem only an alternative of content rather than form. But Eisenstein, whilst maintaining the drive of the narrative, is able to include material that catches the spectators' intellectual as well as their emotional responses. The emphasis on the acts of the epic drama and the use of caesura create spaces in the narrative flow for spectator reflection: the sort of distancing associated with Brecht (see Contexts). The use of certain techniques offers a reinforcement of this reflective space. Some such devices share dual function, thus the battleship's flag works within the plot, but also provides an ideological motif. Other material, like the stone lions is non-diegetic and requires 'reading' by the spectator.

We have here the modernist reflexive techniques that were powerful in

narrative disruptions narrative & form

alternative art forms in the 1920s. The organisation of the narrative and the functions of style within this (see Style) offer something more than the emotional identification found in mainstream melodrama. Eisenstein's concept of pathos aimed at both emotional sympathy and intellectual conviction. It is equally as partisan as the films of Griffith, but offers an intellectual standpoint not found in a film like *Birth of a Nation*.

style

Eisenstein's films were always pushing forward both his practice and his theory of film form. His attitude to questions of style is determined by its position within the overall structure and its function. That function is predominantly political. Eisenstein does not just make films that dramatise Communist politics, as for example Pudovkin's *Mother*. He is seeking to develop specific film forms that give expression to this.

Central to Eisenstein's filmography is montage, the collision of ideas, images and (later) sound out of which grows fresh and new ideas and images. That is a dialectical art, concerned with change, in artistic form and in the audience (see Contexts). Importantly, whilst much comment on Eisenstein's films (especially *Potemkin*) has stressed the use of editing, for Eisenstein himself montage applies to all aspects of the film form.

These are the formal categories of montage that we know:

1 Metric montage
The fundamental criterion for this construction is the *absolute lengths* of the pieces. The pieces are joined together according to their length, in a formula-scheme corresponding to a measure of music. Realisation is in the repetition of these 'measures'.

2 Rhythmic montage
Here, in determining the lengths of the pieces, the content within the frame is a factor possessing equal rights to consideration.

Abstract determination of the piece-lengths gives way to a flexible relationship of the *actual* lengths.

Here the actual length does not coincide with the mathematically determined length of the piece according to a metric formula. Here its practical length derives from the specifics of the piece, and from its planned length according to the structure of the sequence ...

The 'Odessa Steps' sequence in *Potemkin* is a clear example of this ...

'montage ... based on ... characteristic emotional sound'

3 Tonal montage
This term is employed for the first time. It expresses a stage beyond rhythmic montage. ... Here montage is based on the characteristic *emotional sound* of the piece – of its dominant ...

An example: the 'fog sequence' in *Potemkin* (preceding the mass mourning over the body of Vakulinchuk).

Sergei Eisenstein, 1951, pp. 72–6

It will be seen that tonal montage is as much about the composition of the image as the arrangement of images. Eisenstein was to go on to develop ideas about intellectual montage – in *October*; and overtonal montage – in *The Old and the New* and in his sound films. So, bearing in mind Eisenstein's stress on the overall unity of form in film, we can examine the various components of that form. The stylistic elements can be divided into four areas.

mise-en-scène

First we have the composition of what appears in front of the camera. Sets and locations, actors and costumes, movement of various types and lighting. Much of *Potemkin* is filmed at the actual locations, though certain scenes were recreated in specially prepared set-ups and sets. The performers include both actors and ordinary people, some of whom remembered the actual occurrences. And most of the film depends on natural light, amplified by such devices as reflecting mirrors. Rather different from the studio-based product that had emerged as the Hollywood feature. Eisenstein's use of fast and rhythmic editing means that we often notice, primarily, the changing quantity and quality of images, but within these sequences each image is carefully constructed. One facet that quickly becomes apparent is the sense of relentless movement. The continual conflict and development within the narrative are paralleled by continuous conflict and development within the frame. So, on the battleship, when we watch an officer in the mess, just looking:

```
Gilyarovsky stops by a cupboard, opens the
door of it, and inclines his head.
```

movement continues – waves, seagulls, a fluttering flag

> The tables with the tureens upon them swing
> rhythmically on ropes from the ceiling.
> Gilyarovsky shakes his head significantly.
>
> Sergei Eisenstein 1968, p. 35

Even within one of the quietest and most placid scenes, the misty Odessa harbour, movement continues – waves, seagulls, a fluttering flag. This movement reaches its crescendo on the Odessa Steps, when movement within the frame matches changes of the frames.

In both cases patterns can be discerned within these movements. On the ship in Parts I and II, the topographical space is divided between officers and crews, with boundary points, like doorways and stairways. Both individuals and groups move around these areas, paralleling the action. Eisenstein and Tissé use the architecture of the ship to express and symbolise this conflict. Both the commander and the priest occupy dominating positions within the ship scape. The officers are thrown and Vakulinchuk falls from the ship into the sea; whence also the maggoty meat will be consigned.

In Parts III and IV, what we see of Odessa is the port and its environs. All is focused round the jetty with the tent housing Vakulinchuk's body; and the harbour where floats the battleship. The composition creates a series of flows that bring the town to the jetty; and developing flows that carry the citizens from the jetty to the ship.

Eisenstein analyses fourteen shots from this sequence and demonstrates the complexity of the mise-en-scène:

> The scene where the 'good people of Odessa' (as the *Potemkin* sailors addressed their appeal to the population of Odessa) send skiffs with provisions alongside the munitions battleship.
>
> The sending of greetings is constructed on a distinct intersection between two subjects:
>
> 1 The skiffs speed toward the battleship.
>
> 2 The people of Odessa wave.
>
> In the end the two subjects merge.

'The dead man cries for vengeance'

The way in which Eisenstein develops a pattern
which usually reinforces and comments on the
story can be seen towards the end of Part III:
The Dead Man Cries for Vengeance

the greetings of Brothers break down the space

The composition is basically on two planes: depth and foreground. The subjects dominate alternately, advancing to the foreground and pushing one another into the background.

The composition is constructed: (1) on the plastic interaction between both planes (within the shot), (2) on the change in line and form on each plane from shot to shot (by montage).

Taylor, ed., 1988, p. 290

Eisenstein notes the changing positions of subjects within the frame and their changing lines of movement; how architecture, such as columns or a bridge, alters the composition; the contrasting composition of the onlookers; the developing motif of the wave through the arms; and in the thirteenth shot how a specifically ideological image, the flag on the battleship, gives a political point to the movement. (Note, however, that in Mayer, between shots 804 and 813, two shots of the yawls noted by Eisenstein are missing; more significantly, he lists no shot of the flag.)

The congruence of such flows results in the creation and/or reinforcement of the collective, after the mutiny on the ship, and at the town's homage to the dead Vakulinchuk. This congruence emerges again after the tension of the squadron and *Potemkin* approaching each other. As the ships flow forward, the greetings of Brothers break down the space and unite around the rebellious battleship. And the motion is carried forward in the last shot of the film as the prow drives across the screen and into the audience.

The disruption of these collectives comes from alternative spaces. The officers' parts of the ship are carefully demarcated from that of the sailors. Note the fury of the Captain when ordinary seamen attempt to use 'his' gangway. Later such spaces are unseen, in Odessa we do not see the parts of the town housing the military. Even when we see the Opera House targeted after the Odessa Steps, we do not see its surrounds. The admiralty squadron comes out of the undefined spaces of the Black Sea, and (presumably) carries on into them. This connects to presentation of a faceless enemy, a long-standing motif in art, and Eisenstein would have been familiar with many examples.

This continual movement is carefully sited within the locales of ship and harbour. The framing constantly emphasises the power and construction of the ship. There are a significant number of head-on shots of the *Potemkin*'s powerful guns. Much of the movement is in the vertical – the gangways, the ladder – but the mutiny moves into the horizontal of the quarterdeck, and then back to the vertical as the violence erupts. The town seems built round the vertical – stairways – whilst the harbour is built round the horizontal – the jetty.

The tonal qualities of the image also provide a range of hues, and more contrasts. On board ship, the white uniforms of the sailors provide contrast, both with the dark coats of the officers, and the sombre grey of the battleship. In Odessa, tones provide points of contrast within the crowds, from the black of the woman with pince-nez, to the white of the woman with her parasol. These contrasts also work to make characters visible and identifiable in the action. One of the more noticeable contrasts is during the Odessa Steps scene, as the mother and child ascend the steps, the shadows of the troops stand out against a shaft of light running down the steps.

Eisenstein develops visual motifs to accompany those in the narrative (see Narrative). A key example is the pince-nez worn by the ship's surgeon. The surgeon uses this to examine the maggots on the rotten meat: a close-up highlights both the lens and the maggots. When the surgeon gets his just deserts – being thrown overboard – we see a close-up only of the pince-nez, hanging from a rope. This can be described by a term in rhetoric, synecdoche, the part standing in for the whole. The pince-nez also possesses another rhetorical function, that of metonym, an attribute stands in for a thing – in this case, the pince-nez acts as a metaphor for the surgeon's class. This does not exhaust the potential of the pince-nez. The ocular aid reappears, worn by a prominent female character on the steps. After leading a group who plead with the advancing soldiers, she appears to be the victim of the mounted Cossack's sabre. The metonym here is different from that used for the surgeon, yet it also sets up a metaphoric relationship between them: one, possibly, of class; one, possibly, of shared metaphorical blindness. He deliberately fails to see the

a hand-cranked camera of indeterminate speed

maggots; she misguidedly fails to see the relentless purpose of the soldiers (see Contexts, Critical responses).

Another important part of the mise-en-scène are the intertitles (see Cinematic Background). In the silent era they provided plot and character information, dialogue and comments on the story. Eisenstein uses all three: the opening quotation from Lenin (or Trotsky) pronounces the theme of the film; the intertitles that accompany the two sailors present dialogue; whilst the text that opens the lower-deck scene provides information.

camera

Potemkin appears to be filmed using a hand-cranked camera of indeterminate speed. Mayer works on the rough rule of 16fps (frames per second), but it was most likely faster, possibly 20fps. Tissé and his crew lacked most of the accessories that make camera movement so easy today. And they were without the battery of artificial lighting for illumination. The quality of the film image was different as well, shot on nitrate which has a different set of tones from modern safety film, even in black and white. The film also enjoyed a special technique, the hand-painting of the *Potemkin*'s flag, after the mutiny, in red (only found in some prints).

Of the limited range of techniques for silent film, Tissé uses mainly the camera shot, varying the distance, angle, length and lens. *Potemkin* is full of close-ups, often only momentarily on the screen. Over the half the shots on the film are close-ups, and the shortest (on the Odessa Steps) is only five frames. But there is also a range of both mid-shots and long shots; and also long takes, shots that run for longer than the norm. The length seen by the audience will vary depending on projection speed. At 20 frames per second, the shortest shots in *Potemkin* are on screen for a quarter of a second, whilst the longest take over 15 seconds.

As one would expect, the frequency of short shots and close-ups occurs in sequences of dramatic action, as on the Odessa Steps, or the final meeting with the squadron: the predominance of long shots and long takes occurs during passages of relative quiet: carrying Vakulinchuk's body to Odessa, and the morning with the mist.

camera   style

changes of lens rather than changes of camera positions

If there is considerable variation in shot length and camera position, Eisenstein and Tissé also vary the angles used for the camera. One is struck by the strikingly high and low angles that occur from time to time. For example, in the shots of the rushing sailors seen through the gratings of the battleship, the dominant camera looking down on the *mêlée* during the mutiny, or at the sailors' mass meeting in Part V. Most notable is the final low-angle shot of the battleship, bearing down on the audience.

Mayer notes how Tissé has used the same camera position for three shots during the sequence on the quarterdeck, merely changing the lens in order to film the changing subjects:

> [Shot 252   long shot 110 frames]
> (*From above*) The long, open quarterdeck of the Battleship *Potemkin*, seen from amidships, is empty except for three officers who stand in a group. Suddenly, scores of crewmen pour out on the deck in answer to the summons. (*Cut to ...*)
>
> [Shot 253   Long shot 57 frames]
> Sailors begin forming lines on either side of the deck. Two white-trousered officers move to the left. The third officer moves towards the sailors on the right. (*Cut to ...*)
>
> [Photographed from the same position as Shot No. 252 with a longer focus lens for a larger image.]
>
> [Shot 254   Long shot 125 frames]
> (*From above*) The entire crew has now assembled on the quarterdeck and is rapidly forming into three rough lines on either side. More officers appear from beneath the main gun turret.
>
> David Mayer, 1972, p. 67–8

Alexandrov records that Tissé used changes of lens rather than changes of camera positions on the Odessa Steps, partly in order to help the amateur cast relax. This sequence also uses a camera strapped to Alexandrov's body, which explains how they achieved:

48   THE BATTLESHIP POTEMKIN the battleship, bearing down on the audience

The movement of
rebellion drives
into the audience

'another civilian falls through the air'

[Shot 864   mid-shot 11 frames]
The body of another civilian falls through the air, the arc of the
movement blurred by the camera's simultaneous downward thrust.

David Mayer, 1972, p. 175

What are used very little in the film are special effects, in the silent era
normally achieved 'in camera'. There is a superimposition as the captain
threatens the potential mutineers in Part II:

[Shot 289   Long shot 102 frames]
(*From below*) The yardarm stands silhouetted against the sky. After
a moment, six suspended bodies materialise in the air, two hanging
from the upper yardarm and four hanging from the lower yardarm.

David Mayer, 1972, p. 289

There are also two notable dissolves: shot 663 as the steps to the harbour
fill with people; and shot 1048 as the deck of the *Potemkin* strips for
action. The second shot reverses the first, which showed Odessa citizens
leaving their routines to visit Vakulinchuk's funeral: now the sailors are
returning to the battle routines.

Certain shots also form parts of recurring motifs. At the point when the
command is being given to the firing squad Eisenstein inserts shots of the
priest, the battleship's guns and the ship's prow. These last two foreshadow
shots of the ship's guns as *Potemkin* and the squadron approach each
other in Part V, and the final high-angle shot of the prow. These relate to
the question, 'To shoot or not to shoot?' but also set up a motion, which in
the first case is Tsarism bearing down on the mutineers; in the second,
revolutionary brotherhood bearing down on the audience.

editing

We must look for the essence of cinema not in the shots but in the
relationships between shots just as in history we look not at
individuals but at the relationships between individuals,
classes, etc.

Sergei Eisenstein, 1988, p. 79

'movement ... to express mounting emotional intensity'

An overall shot breakdown of *Potemkin* gives little sense of the changing pace of the film because of the changing pattern of type and length of shots. For example, whilst the Odessa Steps sequence seems to be a series of relentless short and close camera set-ups, it actually varies considerably. Using the shot-by-shot analysis in Mayer's breakdown (Mayer, 1972) here is the series of shots that follow the intertitle 'Suddenly ...'

Shot		
854	extreme close-up	7 frames
855	extreme close-up	5 frames
856	extreme close-up	8 frames
857	extreme close-up	10 frames
858	mid-shot	79 frames
859	mid-shot	84 frames
860	long shot	58 frames

Right in the middle of this *mêlée* is a very long take – shot 937 – as the mother bears her child upwards, which runs for 317 frames. This provides a sort of caesura at the heart of the violent sequence. Eisenstein's own description emphasises how the movement of the sequence works:

> Leaving aside the frenzied state of the characters and masses in the scene, let us see how one of the structural and compositional means – *movement* – is used to express mounting emotional intensity.
>
> First, there are *close-ups* of human figures rushing chaotically. Then, *long-shots* of the same scene. The *chaotic movement* is next superseded by shots showing the feet of soldiers as they march *rhythmically* down the steps.
>
> Tempo increases. Rhythm accelerates.
>
> And then, as the *downward* movement reaches its culmination, the movement is suddenly reversed: instead of the headlong rush of the *crowd* down the steps we see the *solitary* figure of a mother carrying her dead son, *slowly* and *solemnly going up the steps*.
>
> *Mass*. Headlong rush. *Downward*. And all of a sudden –

editing style

A *solitary* figure. Slow and solemn. *Going up.* But only for a moment. Then again a *leap in the reverse direction. Downward movement.*

Rhythm accelerates. Tempo increases.

Sergei Eisenstein, 1968, p. 14

Eisenstein's editing of this sequence includes, not just contrasting material in terms of shot length, angle and distance, but contrasts in terms of material that unexpectedly appears. By the 1920s mainstream films, represented by Hollywood, have a whole series of conventions for maintaining continuity. A basic premise was that shots, images, later sounds should match up, at least in the spectator's perception, providing a sense of continuity. However, Eisenstein deliberately inserts shots that break up the continuity. Shots 854 to 857, of a woman's head, following the 'Suddenly ...' title card, do not fit together and do not fit in with preceding or succeeding images, We never know who the woman is or what happened to her. These are jump cuts, the cameras seem to jump around rather than smoothly follow the action. A similar device produces jump cuts from what is known as overlapping montage, the succeeding shot starts at a point before the preceding shot ended. Thus when the Cossack Officer thrusts down his sabre, we see part of the movement twice (shots 1007, 1008, 1009, 1010). Earlier we see the mother returning to rescue her child twice on the same piece of stairway, in successive shots (885–7).

Another variation on this method occurs in Part I, as the young sailor washes the plates for the officers' mess. Having read the inscription (Title-card) 'Give us this day our daily bread', he expresses his anger by smashing the plate. However, in a series of shots we actually see the sailor smash the plate down twice, once to his right and once to his left (shots 240–5).

So, whilst there is a degree of naturalism in the mise-en-scène, and fairly consistent motivation in terms of the narrative, the film does not operate in a strictly realist way. Eisenstein's techniques are designed to arouse what he calls pathos:

'some kind of iron rhythm'

Pathos arouses deep emotions and enthusiasm.

To achieve this, such a work must be built throughout on strong explosive action and constant qualitative changes ...

If we wish the spectator to experience a maximum emotional upsurge, to send him into ecstasy, we must offer him a suitable 'formula' which will eventually excite the desirable emotions in him.

The simplest method is to present on screen a human being in a state of ecstasy, that is, a character who is gripped by some emotion, who is 'beside himself'.

A more complicated and more effective method is the realisation of the main condition of a work of pathos – constant qualitative changes in the action – not through the medium of one character, but through the entire environment. In other words, when everything around him is also 'beside itself'.

Sergei Eisenstein, 1968, p. 13

sound

Potemkin is a silent film, though the intertitles offer some of the information and drama that a modern audience acquires from the soundtrack. In addition, the mise-en-scène, camera and editing are premised on this form. The most obvious example would be the tendency to mime and seemingly over-act in silent film. However, from the earliest screenings exhibitionists used sound and music to add to the experience. Music in particular could heighten the emotions, signal both dramatic and psychological strands to the spectator. *Potemkin* itself was conceived with the idea of fairly grandiose musical accompaniment. In the end, the Soviet version did not enjoy a specially composed score, and there appears to be no record of the actual music used for the Bolshoi premiere. One accompanist has set down his practice:

> I approached Potemkin with trepidation ... The projectionist ran the
> picture for me several times. I began to think of some kind of iron

'They attempted to ban the music'

rhythm that would not spoil the rhythm of the picture itself. It was clear that it demanded symphonic sound, but only a piano was at my disposal. It became my job to find in piano literature something appropriate for the picture.

I struggled for two nights and, finally, having played one of Bach's fugues during the high-powered motion of the ship's engines in the last reel of Potemkin, was astounded by the unexpected rhythmic combination that emerged. Then I began to arrange the fugues of the Well-Tempered Clavier to sequences of the picture. The combination was grandiose.

The great mathematician Bach with his iron inevitability of construction seemed to have something in common with the mathematical construction of the picture.

Lev Arnshtam
in Marshall ed., 1978, p. 107

When the film arrived in Germany a special score was commissioned from the composer Edmund Meisel by the distributors collective, Prometheus:

From 18 March to April 26 Eisenstein and his cameraman Tissé stopped in Berlin in order to be present at the German première. They discussed the different effects of music and Eisenstein and Meisel worked in creative harmony and friendly co-operation. It was very new for an orchestra to produce sound effects from nature, which highlighted the differences between music and sound effects accompanying the synchronised image.

Potemkin was a totally new experience for the German cinema-going public. This film showed that we must struggle to better ourselves even at the expense of our own lives. This unanswered question – whether this sacrifice is worth it increases the tension and Meisel emphasised this by musical climaxes to the point where it was clear to every viewer that a solution must be found here and now. He succeeded in allowing the viewer to directly experience revolutionary pathos. National conservative circles interpreted this as a threat. They attempted to ban the music and show the film without music. *Sudendorf, 1984* trans. Shemilt, 1999

'cacophonies run riot, harmonies grate, crackle, jar'

Marie Seton opines that afterwards Meisel's music was not commonly used outside Germany (though it figures at the London Film Society screening in 1929), and that the distributors circulated recommended sheet music. At least one New York screening enjoyed the score and produced one of the few critical responses to the music:

> ... the New York presentation of *Potemkin* ... The music was almost passed over entirely by the critics of the metropolitan press, which was a mistake, for the score is as powerful, as vital, as galvanic and electrifying as the film. It is written in the extreme modern vein, cacophonies run riot, harmonies grate, crackle, jar; there are abrupt changes and shifts in the rhythm; tremendous chords crashing down, dizzy flights of runs, snatches of half-forgotten melodies, fragments, a short interpolation of jazz on a piano and melody in the central portion of the film – when the people of Odessa stand on the steps waving to the sailors on the cruiser Potemkin and others go out on fishing boats with provisions for them, – that is one of the loveliest I have ever heard.
>
> *Herman G. Weinberg, 1928*
> in Marshall ed., 1978, p.127

This review has the merit of highlighting the modernist style of Meisel's score, a modernist style to which we, years later, are more accustomed.

Of course, whilst the changes in the film varied due to censorship, the accompanying music could vary according to performance. Eisenstein 'complained that, with the Meisel music, we had turned his picture into an opera' (Ivor Montagu, 1967, p. 37, on the London Film Society screening). One suggestion is that the Meisel score, and the accommodation in film projection speed, altered Eisenstein's intended rhythms for certain sequences.

Presumably there were huge variations for audiences, some viewing with just the projector whirr in the background; others with a piano of varying qualities; others still with an orchestra, possibly running counter to the rhythms of Eisenstein's construction.

'the only authentic film worthy of the Soviet land'

director's cut

The musical score is one important issue in the varying prints of Eisenstein's film. A director's cut in the sense we use it in the 1990s does not exist. The existing versions of the film's script do not really resolve questions. The officially published script (Sergei Eisenstein, 1968) is obviously produced after the filming. There is an incomplete shooting script, but reference to that shows that the film developed considerably during the production. And there are several different prints available. Ian Christie points out that:

> it makes little sense to search for a unique original or authentic version ... four distinct processes of textual variation can be identified:
>
> 1 politically motivated alterations before and after domestic release;
>
> 2 foreign distributors' changes, as demanded by local censorship, but also arising from translation, projection practice and commercial judgement;
>
> 3 Eisenstein's own revisions when the opportunity or need presented itself;
>
> 4 deliberate 'modernisation', especially when synchronised sound was added (including step-printing).
>
> Christie & Taylor eds., 1993, pp. 8–9

Step-printing means adding frames, usually one for every second frame, to 'stretch' the print from running at a silent speed to 24fps. If this film was actually shot to run at over 20fps, like Eisenstein's films, the result is to alter the rhythms of the piece radically. The differences apparent in prints were a source of complaint in the 1920s:

> Who would have thought that the only authentic film worthy of the Soviet land, *The Battleship Potemkin*, would have had such a fate?
>
> ... Briefly speaking, success abroad so turned the head of our film dealers that, with only the briefest consideration, they

sold the negative to Germany, keeping only the right to retain copies.

And in the meantime, the limited quantity of copies located here in the USSR is getting worn out – the best of these have only 40% serviceability left.

Kransnaia Gazeta, Leningrad, 28 October, 1926
in Marshall ed., 1978, p. 105

The German print was censored, as were practically all the prints in circulation in the west. In addition to this, there appear to have been enforced changes by the Soviet authorities.

Research I have done indicates that this first version of *The Battleship Potemkin* contained an epigraph which came immediately after the act-title '1. Men and Maggots.' The latter faded out or dissolved into the epigraph, and then the epigraph faded out and was directly followed by five shots of waves crashing onto a breakwater. It was worded as follows (my translation):

The spirit of Insurrection hovered over the Russian land. Some enormous and mysterious process was taking place in countless hearts. The individual was dissolving in the mass and the mass was dissolving in the outburst.

This epigraph came from Lev D. Trotsky article 'The Red Navy', which had been printed many times ... [he notes a later sentence in the original runs]

It was borne ahead like a wave of the sea driven by the storm.

Stephen P. Hill
in Marshall ed., 1978, p.76

Hill quotes Montagu as a source that this epigraph was in the version screened in London in 1929. But later prints contain,

'Revolution is the only lawful, equal, effectual war. It was in Russia that this war was declared and begun.' Lenin

(Hill notes that the quotation is from an article written by Lenin in 1905.)

a sound image counterpoint

By 1956, even Lenin's epigraph is changed. The 1956 version reads:

> Russia is going through a great historical movement. The
> Revolution has flared up. Its flames spreading wider and wider
> enveloping new areas, new strata of society. The proletariat
> stands in the van of the militant forces of the revolution.

Russian Classics video

On this occasion the Soviet authorities have added a voice-over, and extra titles, which seem to be about clarifying plot detail. For example, a voice-over with English subtitles informs the viewer about the Russo-Japanese war and the workers' strike in Odessa. The voice-over reappears at the end of the film with sound effects, e.g., cheering accompanying the joyful sailors. In between, an extra intertitle informs us that Matushenko and Vakulinchuk are 'acting on instructions from an underground organisation'. The chapter titles preceding each part have been removed, so that the narrative has a continuous flow. This version appears post-German censored, as there are several important shots changed or missing: the woman's head at the top of the steps (854–7) has been separated from the title 'Suddenly ...' by the insertion of shots of the troops firing; the shooting of the mother and child; and the Cossack officer and the pince-nez woman's face (shots 1007–12) are completely missing. Steven Hill notes that the new Lenin quotation is from volume 7 of his collected works, and suggests the earlier quotation clashed with the 'World Peace' front of the 1950s. The soundtrack includes not the score by Meisel, but a new score by Nikolai Kryukov, inferior to the earlier. In the 1970s a more complete and visually improved print was 'stretched' and received an accompanying score arranged by Shostakovich from his symphonic music.

Rather than choice, availability will probably determine what a reader can view. The silent prints are better and closer to Eisenstein. The differing intertitles are historically interesting, but the cuts by censors have a greater impact on the film.

And Meisel's score is best, his music interacts with Eisenstein's images in a sound image counterpoint (Ian Christie & Richard Taylor eds, 1993). (See Filmography for availability.)

contexts

cultural & ideological

The 1920s, following the Great War, was turbulent but exciting. Most significantly, the Soviet Revolution, for the first time for over a hundred years, had seen the overturning of the international *status quo*. For the establishments it provided a demon excessively more threatening than would its successor in the post-Second World War divisions. For the oppressed and exploited, the majority, it existed as a beacon of light, as a real, tangible utopia that was possible for all. Much of the internal politics of the new Soviet Union were reactive to this situation: how to fend off the capitalist enemy, how to fulfil its responsibilities to the world proletariat and oppressed peoples.

Contemporary post-collapse views emphasise the changing responses of the Soviet Union very much in terms of personalities, especially Joseph Stalin. Nineteen-twenties' Communists saw it in ideological and political terms. Lenin died in 1924, leaving a set of contradictory policies. There was Soviet power and command of the State, but a society full of both feudal and capitalist relations. Treading the unknown path of Socialist Construction led to the emergence of political antagonisms. A key factor in this struggle was less the character of Stalin or even Trotsky (the two best-known members of the opposing factions) than the changing nature of the party. As a new State machine emerged, its functionaries joined the party: frequently they were not proletarian, but petty bourgeois (middling strata), the people who possessed the necessary skills for the work at hand. From this stems changing political interests and a changing political line. The Dictatorship of the Proletariat has an ambiguous ring even in the 1920s, more so in the 1930s. Control and defence become abiding concerns of the rising class. In the cultural sphere, Lenin's willingness to allow a huge variety of forms and experimentation, which he nevertheless often strongly attacked, gives way to an increasingly preceptorial line.

Prior to this, during the Civil War and early NEP period, Soviet culture was a veritable bazaar of new ideas and new forms. In this it reflected the wider world of culture. The period is full of new cultural 'isms', new ideas, new theories. Within Soviet culture there were a number of important lines of cultural theory and practice. Eisenstein was involved in these through his career, first in theatre then in cinema; but also through the general argument and discussion around cultural practice. From the point of view of this films the following are key factors:

■ Techne-centred thought – 'Techne is Aristotle's term for the unity of theory and practice within a skilled activity. Any craft, artistic or not, includes not only practices but also a systematic knowledge underlying them' (Bordwell, 1993, p. 35; see Chapters 1 and 3 for excellent summaries of the various theories).

■ Constructivism – emphasised art in terms of the machine and material form, 'an objective or task performed according to a particular system, for which purpose particular materials have been organised and worked in a manner corresponding to their inherent characteristics' (Bordwell, 1993, p. 35).

■ In acting there was the theory and practice around Meyerhold, the dominant figure in revolutionary theatre. 'He advocated the principle of "bio-mechanics", that is, translating dramatic emotion into archetypal gestures, the abolition of individual characterisation and the emphasis on the "class kernel" of the dramatic presentation. In some ways he anticipated Bertolt Brecht in desiring the spectators never to forget they were in the theatre ...' (Bergan, 1997, pp. 68–9). He was another strong influence on Eisenstein, who also attended his classes at the state School for Stage Direction.

■ Attractions – in both theatre and cinema there was a tendency both to excite and shock spectators. This is apparent in other Proletcult productions and in the work of FEKS (Factory of the Eccentric Actors), who proclaimed, 'the streets bring revolution to art. Our street mud is circus,

cultural & ideological

A crescendo
in the film's
pathos

some artists wanted to junk all prior 'bourgeois' art

cinema, music-hall!' (Bergan, 1997, p. 76). Eisenstein maintains: 'An attraction (in our diagnosis of theatre) is any aggressive moment in theatre, i.e. any element that subjects the audience to emotional or psychological influence ...' (Taylor, 1988, p. 34).

■ Behaviourism – ideas from Pavlov and his associates circulated. This produced theories that behaviour and responses could be predicted; tied to bio-mechanics, some suggested sets of movements could be tabulated and artworks constructed to stimulate audience in the desired way. Eisenstein continues on about attractions, 'verified by experience and mathematically calculated to produce specific emotional shocks in the spectator in their proper order within the whole' (Taylor, ibid.).

■ All this was in a context of revolutionary change. Some artists wanted to junk all prior 'bourgeois' art. Certainly the new art had to be different. It had to serve the ideological needs of the revolution, it had to address the interests of the ordinary people and it had to address them directly. Eisenstein's mathematically calculated 'shocks provide the only opportunity of perceiving the ideological aspect of what is being shown, the final ideological conclusion' (Taylor, ibid.).

In this context a work's function became an overriding concern. Tied to this was an expectation that by combining theory and practice artists could develop the forms necessary to fulfil these tasks. Dialectics was another central concept. It has a range of interpretations, but tends to centre on change as the motor of history, and analyses of the underlying class and economic conflicts that drive social change forward. Dialectical thinking received an injection of discussion in the 1920s; its emphasis on a conflict model fitted well with the experiences and events of the Soviet Revolution. It also made sense of the world of conflict in the relations, internal and external, of the USSR. It became a key concept in both theorising and constructing the new socialist art.

Eisenstein, whilst bringing his own talents and preoccupations, was firmly within this milieu. Many of his articles argue fiercely and sometimes dogmatically about both the form and function of art. His stress on the unity of a work of art is a question of subordinating it to the key function.

industrial institutions

His attention to minute detail of form and style is part of this relentless quest for the correct forms to fulfil these functions.

His film career is, in one sense, a series of attempts to apply theoretical concepts to the production of artworks. The emphasis on theory would increase later in his career, but it is there in the 1920s. *Strike* was a series of experiments by a young film-maker. *Potemkin* is intended to be more disciplined, but also a development onwards from the agitational film. And *October* and *The Old and The New* introduced further developments on *Potemkin*.

industrial institutions

In the Civil War period Soviet power was primarily concerned with producing newsreels and 'Agitki', agitational dramas and documentaries. The Agit Trains, which scoured the vast countryside, took these and other political arts and crafts to the peasantry. With peace, more ambitious possibilities were opened up. As the newest form of art and communication, film was seen by the Bolsheviks as a key weapon. But they were concerned both about the content offered by film and the form in which this was offered. Between 1920 and 1924 film production crept up from eleven per annum to 157. In the same period Soviet control was increasingly exerted on the industry. In 1923 Goskino (Central State Photographic and Cinematographic Enterprise) established a state monopoly of production and distribution. The system allowed the importation and screening of films from the capitalist west; both Douglas Fairbanks and Charlie Chaplin were popular stars in this period. However, the control of distribution meant that a proportion of the profits from this exhibition was funnelled back into state production – a production that was to differ increasingly from the standard product from the west. Those Soviet films that were exported were used to raise the cost of equipment and stock.

Sergei Eisenstein was one amongst a group of mainly young film-makers, who bought a new vitality, political content and radical style to cinema. Nineteen twenty-five was in some ways their *annus mirabilis*.

the incredible potency of montage

■ **Yakov Protazanov** directed *His Call* (*Yevo prizyv*); Protazanov had worked in the Russian film industry before the revolution. He had joined the pro-Tsarist emigration abroad for a time but, like a number of artists and intellectuals, returned as the new society stabilised itself. Whilst both the style and content of his films changed, he represented a link with the earlier silent cinema.

■ **Lev Kuleshov** directed *The Death Ray* (*Luch smerti*). This was a veritable compendium of new techniques, in particular the fast and dramatic juxtaposition of shots achieved through edits, the new style of montage. Kuleshov had worked in the Pre-revolutionary cinema, as a set designer. During the Civil War period he worked on documentaries. In the early days of the revolution, when both film equipment and film stock was non-existent, Kuleshov and his workshop team experimented with his ideas of film editing. These famous experiment included: 'a more complex experiment: we shot a complete scene. Khokhlova and Obolensky acted in it. We filmed them in the following way: Khokhlova is walking along Petrov Street in Moscow near the 'Mostorg' store. Obolensky is walking along the embankment of the Moscow River – at a distance of about two miles away. They see each other, smile, and begin to walk towards one another. Their meeting is filmed at the Boulevard Prechistensk. This boulevard is in an entirely different section of the city. They clasp hands, with Gogol's monument as a background, and look – at the White House! – for at this point, we cut in a segment from an American film, *The White House in Washington*. ... This particular scene demonstrated the incredible potency of montage, which actually appeared so powerful that it was able to alter the very essence of the material. From this scene, we came to understand that the basic strength of cinema lies in montage, because with montage it becomes possible both to break down and to reconstruct, and ultimately remake material' (Levaco, 1974, p. 52). Kuleshov's theory and practice were to be enormously influential in the 1920s' Soviet Cinema. In particular his ideas were taken up and developed by Eisenstein.

■ **Dziga Vertov** directed *Leninist Film-truth*, number 21 in his series *Kino-Pravda*. Vertov was also a theoretician and practitioner. He was committed to documentary and newsreel, rejecting the artifice of the story drama.

production history

The history of Kino-Eye has been a relentless struggle to modify the course of world cinema, to place in cinema production a new emphasis of the "unplayed" film over the play-film, to substitute the document for mise-en-scène, to break out of the proscenium of the theatre and to enter the arena of life itself' (Jay Leyda, 1960, p. 176).

■ **Vsevolod Pudovkin**, another master of editing, directed *Chess Fever* (*Shakhamtnaya goryachka*), and filmed the actual International Chess Tournament in Moscow to produce a fictional comedy. He also started filming *Mother*, from the Gorky novel, a film which came out in 1926.

■ And Sergei Eisenstein had two films premièred.

production history

The original commission for the 1905 commemorations envisaged a large-scale epic film depicting the whole range of the revolution of that year. In March 1925 the Official State Committee of the Presidium of the Central Executive Committee of the USSR passed a resolution for

> an important film, presented within a special setting, with oratorical, musical (orchestral and choral) and dramatic accompaniment, according to a specially written text, in order that thereby the twentieth anniversary of the 1905 Revolution should be solemnly celebrated'
>
> Marshall ed., 1978, p. 53

By April, Eisenstein is writing to his mother, 'At Goskino I will most probably be shooting the film *The Year 1905*, extremely interesting material ...' (Herbert Marshall ed., 1978, p. 55).

In June a conference records:

> An exposition of the content and structure of the film scenarios dedicated to the events of 1905:
>
> (a) Prepared by N. Shutko on the general theme of the events of 1905;

'an attempt to get to grips with the dynamism of the epoch'

(b) Written by Schegolev on the theme 'January 9, 1905.' (Com. K. I. Shutko).

Resolution: That the spectacle approved by the Commission shall be produced as a cinema film 1905, based on the scenario prepared by Com. N. Shutko.

Marshall ed., 1978, p. 57

(*Ninth of January* was also filmed, but failed to make an impact on the scale of *Potemkin*.) There was also a proposal to commission musical accompaniment by Prokofiev, which came to nought.

Eisenstein and Nina [Shutko] then worked on a script for the original conception. He recalls:

the immeasurably wide flood of events of 1905 and putting them down on countless sheets of paper ...

More than simply an array of typical facts and episodes: it was an attempt to get to grips with the dynamism of the epoch, to feel its pulse, the sinews within that connected the different events.

In brief, an extensive summary of that preparatory work, without which the feeling of 1905 as a whole could not pour itself into each particular episode of *Potemkin*.

Taylor, 1995, pp. 150–1

However, this probably overambitious epic was transformed by events outside the official production schedule. Alexandrov recalled:

We began shooting in Leningrad during the summer of 1925. It was absolutely essential that we complete work by December 31, 1925. But, by the end of the summer, Agadzhanova still had not finished her scenario. The weather was very bad in Leningrad, so we took the advice of Kapinchinsky, the Leningrad film director and left for Odessa. There Eisenstein decided his movie would treat only the *Potemkin* mutiny, which until then had been a single episode disposed of in three pages of an endless scenario.

production history

> We went to the London Hotel, where Eisenstein wrote a short outline. We met numerous witnesses to the events, and we often improvised as we shot ...
>
> *Interview with G. V. Alexandrov*
> Marshall ed., 1978, p. 70

D.J. Wenden notes a suggestion that Sergei Tret'yakov, dramatist and an associate of Eisenstein's at Proletkult, contributed to the scenario (K.R.M. Short ed., 1981). Tret'yakov was in Odessa during the filming. And he had already drafted a play, which appears to have a similar structure to *Potemkin*. It is set in China and involves the conflict between a British gunboat and local Chinese people, played out between the warship and the harbour. Tret'yakov is credited as joint author of the intertitles, so it is possible – but not conclusive that this was so.

Eisenstein comments on the changing shape of the script:

> And so, line by line, the screenplay became scene after scene. Because it was not the sketchy notes of a libretto that supplied the true emotional depth, but that complex of feelings that blew up like a whirlwind in a series of vivid images at the mere passing mention of the events that I had recently relived. ...
>
> How they reproved scriptwriters for daring to express themselves in this way! ...
>
> Without being deflected from the sense of truth, we were able to indulge any whim or fancy, bringing it into any events or scene we wished even if it were not in the original libretto (like the 'Odessa Steps'!), and any unforeseeable detail (such as the mist at the funeral scene!)
>
> Taylor ed., 1995, p. 152

Taylor points out in a footnote (pp. 814–5) that:

> The term 'ironclad screenplays' [zheleznye stsenarii] was used in the mid-1920s and reflected the ideas of those who felt that the screenplay should encompass every detail of the film, before it went into production, and that in production the screenplay should be strictly adhered to. E. [Eisenstein] counterposed to this

'the small moustache, pointed beard ... Shifty eyes'

> his own notion of an 'emotional screenplay' or libretto, which
> would confine itself to the broad outlines of the film and permit
> the director a very considerable degree of scope for innovation and
> creative freedom.

Eisenstein always thoroughly researched any topic or story he planned to
dramatise.

> During the first few days, he delved into the history of the mutiny
> of the sailors. ... He found a series of sketches by a French artist
> who had witnessed the massacre on the Odessa stairway. He talked
> to survivors whose accounts gave him the 'feel' of what had
> happened twenty years before. 'The only thing I need is contact
> with the people,' he said later. 'How many times have I gone out,
> with sketches and drawings, and then, on finding myself among
> the masses, on feeling their nearness, I have changed the idea
> completely. It is they, in their spontaneity, who actually imprint on
> the film the great tone of reality.
>
> Seton, 1960, p. 75

Eisenstein's use of typage meant he was constantly looking out for the
visually suitable face and form.

> one of the most important figures, structurally, was the Doctor. ...
> I began appraising the camera assistants.
> One of them was short, puny.
> It was the boilerman of the hotel in Sebastopol where we were
> staying. We killed time there between shoots. ...
> At this point my thoughts came to a standstill: the skinny
> boilerman suddenly appeared in a new light as I reappraised him.
> I thought of his physical attributes, not vis-à-vis the work he has
> to do, but his appearance.
> The small moustache, pointed beard ...
> Shifty eyes ...
> I imagined them behind pince-nez on their little ribbon.
> I mentally swapped his oil-stained cap for a hat of an army
> medic ...

'the misty bay ... an endless apple orchard in blossom'

And at that moment when we got on deck to start the shoot, my thoughts became a reality. The ship's medical orderly subjected the infested meat to a cursory squint through the twin lenses of his pince-nez – but a moment earlier he had been an honest boilerman, hired as an assistant ...

Taylor ed., 1995, pp. 167–8

Several important scenes resulted from changes Eisenstein made during the filming, with consequent changes to the 'non-ironclad' script. Two improvisations in the film resulted from visual stimuli seen by Eisenstein:

There was also the famous mist.

One misty morning in the harbour ...

The mist lay like cotton wool over the mirror-like surface of the bay.

The reality is more prosaic.

The mist over the bay meant simply enforced inactivity – ...

Anyway, there was no filming.

Inactivity.

A day off.

It cost three roubles fifty to hire a boat.

Tissé, Alexandrov and I sailed across the misty bay as if crossing an endless apple orchard in blossom.

Taylor ed., 1995, pp. 169–70

In a longer passage Eisenstein explains how the central sequence on the steps came about, but also delves deeply into his approach to film-making.

The lions. The mist.

The third lucky find was the Odessa Steps themselves.

I always believe that nature, one's surroundings, the set at the point of filming and even the exposed footage at the point of montage, are all more intelligent than the author and director.

the very core of the film's organic substance

Being able to listen and comprehend what nature, or the unforeseen, is hinting at in the scene that was conceived in your thoughts; being able to detect what the cut film is saying on the splicing table as it lives out its own life on the screen (and this can be at some remove from the parameters of what was intended) – this is a great blessing and a great art ... additionally, you must be flexible in your choice of means for realising the concept. ...

The scene of the slaughter on the Odessa Steps was not indicated in any of my preparatory notes for the screenplay.

The scene was born out of a momentary spontaneous encounter. ...

The actual 'flight' of steps led to the planning of the scene, and its upward flight set my directing off on a new flight of fancy.

And I think that the crowd's headlong 'flight' down the steps was no more than the material realisation of those first feelings that I experienced when I came face to face with the actual steps.

Anyway, apart from that, only one other thing assisted me: somewhere, in my memory, was a vague recollection of a picture from a magazine *L'Illustration* in 1905, where a horseman, shrouded in smoke, slashed at someone with his sabre, on a flight of steps.

One way or another, the scene on the Odessa Steps became a crucial scene, the very core of the film's organic substance and general structure.

Taylor ed., 1995, pp. 171–3

And the final images from this part of the film: 'The "lion leaping to its feet" was a lucky find we made in Alupka, where we had gone merely to rest from filming on one of our days off' (Richard Taylor ed., 1995, pp. 168–9).

The filming, especially on the steps, required great inventiveness, and demonstrates the degree to which Eisenstein relied on his colleagues, most especially Eduard Tissé:

Eisenstein and Tissé worked with magnificent energy and inspiration. They infected everyone and everything with their own

production history

feelings. 'They went tirelessly up, and down this stairway of 120 steps all the time finding new and different possibilities of expression.' By the standards of Hollywood 1925, their technical equipment was exceedingly primitive. But they overcame these limitations by original experiments. They used mirror reflectors for the first time in the Soviet Union, and Tissé devised out-of-focus photography. In order to shoot the downward movement on the steps, invention was resorted to. A moveable wagonette, large enough to hold the camera, Tissé, Eisenstein and his assistants, was constructed. It was shuttled up and down alongside the stairs on specially built wooden rails. By this means the camera could follow the downward motion of the soldiers and the crowd on the steps.

Seton, 1960, p. 79

Note, one of the reflecting mirrors provides a non-diegetic prop behind the student seen at the foot of the Odessa Steps.

Over all this activity still hovered the deadline enforced by the actual anniversary. Eisenstein left early for Moscow in order to edit the film, leaving Alexandrov with Tissé to shoot some final scenes, a second unit. Theirs is the famous final shot of the battleship's prow, achieved by moving the camera underneath the stationery ship. Eisenstein spent about two weeks editing the mass of material, some 16,000 metres of film, down to a final cut of 1,640 metres. He was still editing when the première screening opened, Alexandrov carrying reels to the Bolshoi Theatre on his motor-cycle. His last trip also carried Eisenstein, who only arrived during the actual performance.

The Bolshoi Theatre resounded with applause which roared like grapeshot through the semicircular corridors. I was in a corridor, worried not only for the film's sake, but because of the spit. The last part of the film was held together by spit [due to the last-minute editing].

I clambered higher and higher, from the stalls to the dress circle, from tier to tier, as the excitement mounted. I listened anxiously and eagerly for individual bursts of applause.

'miracle! the spit held!'

Until the auditorium exploded with tumultuous cheers like grapeshot – the first time. That was the sequence with the red flag.

A second time the 'Potemkin's' guns thundered against the headquarters of the general staff in response to the slaughter in Odessa ...

The film would come apart at any moment!

The projector would send fragments flying ...

The rhythm of the film's finale would be broken.

And suddenly, imagine! A miracle! the spit held!

The picture raced to its conclusion.

We could not believe our eyes later, in the editing suite. Without the slightest effort we separated those minute pieces that earlier had adhered to each other with miraculous strength as they sped through the projector! ...

Taylor ed., 1995, pp. 181–2

distribution

The film went into general distribution on 19 January 1926. Detailed records for the period do not exist: however, the Soviet authorities did carry out some comparisons with an example of imported films.

Among the public there has occurred a decisive change in favour of Soviet films.

... The Soviet Battleship Potemkin and the American Robin Hood [ran continuously] for twelve days [in Moscow]:

In the First Theatre Goskino:

The Battleship Potemkin	29,458 people
Robin Hood	21,281

In the Second Theatre Goskino

The Battleship Potemkin	39,405 people
Robin Hood	33, 960 people

Kino Gazeta, 16 February 1926
in Herbert Marshall ed., 1978, p. 101

distribution

The film opened simultaneously at twelve Moscow cinemas, with special attractions: the First Goskino cinema was decked out like a battleship. But actual audiences were probably less impressive than the figures suggest and *Potemkin*'s claims to popularity are less than clear cut. For instance, *Robin Hood* was being reshown after *Potemkin* had been taken off. And another Soviet film *The Bear's Wedding* [*Medvezh'ya svad'ba*] played to 64,000 people in a similar period. In many cases *Potemkin* was restricted to worker's clubs, organised by the state, rather than being shown in commercially run cinemas. A frequent comment is that *Potemkin* was not popular with ordinary audiences.

The real sensation occurred when the film was released in Germany in May 1926. Setting a pattern for its release around the world, the film immediately ran into censorship problems. It was only a campaign by intellectuals and liberals that prevented an outright ban.

> I The resolution of the Berlin Censorship Committee of 24 March 1926 on #12595 is revoked.
>
> II The film is released for open exhibition in the territory of the German state; however, it cannot be shown to young audiences.
>
> The following sequences are forbidden.
>
> In Part II, subtitle 22:
>
> 'O Lord! Punish the disobedient and make the sinner listen to reason!'
>
> In Part III, after subtitle 1:
>
> Wrapped up in a sail, an officer is dragged by the legs as he tries to grasp at the deck. Length 1.90 m.
>
> They throw the officer overboard; he surfaces again. Length 1.34 m.
>
> Close-up of a man beating the legs of another man with the butt of his rifle. The other falls in the water, swims. Length 3 m.
>
> The ship's doctor, being dragged along headfirst, tries to grab hold of a rope. Length 3.50 m.
>
> Close-up of the ship's ladder with a soldier's legs and an officer's arms trying to grab the ladder. Length 0.80 m.

In Part V, after subtitle 1:

Close-up of a man falling on the steps of the staircase. Length 1.95 m.

Close-up of three women sitting on the steps of the staircase huddling together. Length 0.60 m.

Close-up of man who, having fallen on the staircase, is stepped on by the Cossacks. Length 0.70 m.

Child, situated next to his mother on the steps of the staircase, is injured in one of the volleys. Close-up of the profuse bleeding of the child and his legs, over which other people are running, and, further, of the head of the child, which a mother steps over. (It was permitted to show how the mother lifts the child and moves towards the Cossacks with the child in her arms.) Length 1.89 m.

After subtitle 3:

The woman with the child in her arms falls under the Cossack's fire; the Cossacks walk past the woman at the bottom of the staircase. Length 2.55 m.

A man climbs up the railings, in front of which a great number of wounded lie, and falls, struck down by bullets. Length 0.85 m.

Close-up of a woman's arm grasping her belt. Length 1.47 m.

At the same time as the woman falls backwards on the steps of the staircase, the carriage with the baby begins to roll down the steps below. The man who tries to climb over the balustrade is hit by bullets. The baby carriage rolls by the corpses and overturns. Close-up of the Cossack's head as he swings a whip. Length 9.50 m.

III All expenses connected with the suit fall to the Plaintiff's account ...

Chief Film Censorship Committee, Berlin, 10 April 1926
in Marshall ed., 1978, pp. 120–1

(Note the print appears to be in a different reel order, the Part III above is actually Part II and the Part V is actually Part IV in Eisenstein's descriptions.)

Part of the concern of the German authorities was the fear of the film's impact on ordinary soldiers and sailors. Germany was only a few years

audience

away from a failed revolution in 1919. On at least one occasion curfews were ordered in garrison towns, and military police posted to prevent serving men attending the screenings.

These sorts of cuts were typical of how the film was treated abroad. It meant that the audiences saw only a paler version of Eisenstein's masterpiece. In particular the censors cut out crucial images in the Odessa Steps sequence.

Apart from galvanising the censors and military authorities, the German exhibition put *Potemkin* firmly on the artistic map. It became the talking point of both intellectual and political circles. Large audiences turned out for all sorts of screenings, presumably many of them attracted by its notoriety as much as by its politics.

In December 1926 it arrived in New York, heralded by Douglas Fairbanks and Mary Pickford, who had seen it on a tour of the Soviet Union. Eisenstein and his film had become possibly the most famous cinematic event of the mid 1920s, and in places and circles where cinema was not an accepted artistic medium. The international reception impacted back in the Soviet Union. There is a record of Mayakovsky berating the officials at Goskino for their cavalier treatment of *Potemkin*. There is the problem (noted earlier) of the sale of the negatives to the German distributors. More positively, the response and consequent profits appear to have impacted on the Party support and resources provided for the new style of cinema. (see Kristin Thompson in Christie & Taylor eds, 1993, pp. 53–63.)

audience

It seems clear, that apart from possibly Germany, *Potemkin* was not a popular film in the mainstream sense. The audiences who did watch *Potemkin*, and who were both amazed and captured by the film, were most likely more 'advanced workers'. An assumption of Bolshevik ideology was that some proletarians, advanced elements, had greater class consciousness. They could be offered complex political material: propaganda. The less advanced elements, the mass, would need simpler political material: agitation. *October* would be a clear example of complex propaganda for the advanced, whilst *Alexander Nevsky*, and socialist

one poor distributor was visited and cautioned by the police

realism material in general, restricts itself to the agitational. *Potemkin*, in fact, combines both propaganda and agitation, with the Odessa Steps being clearly agitational. Eisenstein, and the party, would have hoped it would appeal to the masses. But the more propagandistic elements, like the way 'attractions' disrupt the continuity, were often found difficult.

When the film arrived abroad, it was perceived as propaganda in the capitalist sense, i.e. consciously propagating a particular (one-sided?) point of view. However, the distinctive way in which it presented its politics, the attractions and disruptions, found an immediate response. For class-conscious proletarians the film offered class politics in a clearly alternative form to the dominant ideology found in the Hollywood film. For intellectuals the film offered the alternative form from the mainstream which was exciting, even if the politics were not necessarily shared or adopted.

The latter group were more likely to be able to enjoy the film than the former. There was economic censorship: *Potemkin* was frequently shown in prestige cinemas with orchestras, and probably was expensive viewing. More to the point, the censors were most worried by the group whom the film addressed most directly: oppressed workers, the poor and dispossessed. In Britain, despite the ban, it was possible to show the film in a private society if the local authority approved. In 1929 the predominantly middle class and intellectual Film Society was able to organise a screening. Requests for the same licence from working-class organisations for private showings were turned down flat. In fact, it is reported that one poor distributor was visited and cautioned by the police merely for running the print for the staff at his offices. In the 1930s the Kino Distribution Section of the Workers' Theatre Movement had more success in screening the film. When the film was available for the ordinary but class-conscious workers, its impact was notable. The reception at the Bolshoi was repeated frequently at subsequent screenings.

Foreign audiences probably enjoyed a wide range of readings. Eisenstein's construction of the film aimed at very precise effects on the spectator. This is true both of his montage in terms of cutting the film, and also in terms of rhetorical devices and motifs. But he was well aware of the limitations imposed on the film experience by cultural, class and ideological factors. 'It is quite clear that for a worker and a former cavalry officer the chain of associations set off by seeing a meeting broken up and a corresponding emotional effect in contrast to the material which frames this incident, will be somewhat different' (Taylor ed., 1988, pp. 41–2). Later Eisenstein discusses a particular example, the slaughter of a bull in *Strike*, an extra-diegetic effect, and notes that the class-basis of an audience will affect the reading. He believes workers will make the correct association, whilst others may regard it as shocking and unacceptable (as western censors did with the deaths on the steps in *Potemkin*). Eisenstein's ire at the London screening was partly due to the audience laughing at the Stone Lions. This may have been due to an incorrect projection speed, but it is also possibly due to the 'sophistication' of a nonproletarian audience.

influence

Potemkin did not just create a sensation, it quickly exerted a powerful influence on the developing silent cinema: an influence that continued into the sound era.

There is no doubt of the influence on Soviet film. In terms of montage this fed into other currents, including Kuleshov, Vertov and Pudovkin's work. When socialist realism arrived in the 1930s, montage fell out of favour as an example of formalism. But socialist realism itself was heavily dependent on the epic dramatisation and characterisation that Eisenstein developed in *Potemkin*. His own *Alexander Nevsky* owes much to the epic style of *Potemkin*, whilst its montage is perforce much subtler and picks up on aspects other than just the editing. Ironically, when socialist realism became the stereotype to be overthrown, film-makers like Tarkovsky then returned to the essential elements of Eisenstein's montage as a basic block in their attack. Eisenstein towers over Mosfilm as Griffith towers over Hollywood.

In the western commercial world of film, as was so often the case, it was those aspects of Eisenstein that could be accommodated within the existing structures that were copied – in fact, in exactly the same way that Hollywood used Rubens and Raphael. In the 1930s many Hollywood films

'no parboiled theatricals, no glare of studio lights'

contained montage sequences which featured the fast-changing editing tactics of *Potemkin*, but totally without its modernist disruptions, fitting seamlessly into the dominant narrative. An Hungarian film-maker, Slavko Vorkapich, became the resident montage expert for 1930s' Hollywood. He produced a large number of short, fast-edited sequences inserted into studio vehicles, particularly at MGM and Columbia.

In art cinema Eisenstein's influence is even more pervasive. In fact, fast and more complex editing had already been seen in European cinema: Abel Gance's *La Roue* and Fritz Lang's *Dr Mabuse* offering two examples. And the independent cinemas of different political hues also felt the impact.

> There is another point besides the brilliance of the cinema storytelling which might be raised in connection with *Potemkin*. The film is a 'natural film' in the sense of the newsreel being a natural film. It has the authenticity of life about it. In the entire continuity it seems there is not a single actor or studio effect. The Russian government, it is said, gave the director, Eisenstein, carte blanche. Out he went and commandeered ships and crews and entire populations and worked from life. Some persistently maintain that the screen will make its greatest achievements working from life; and *Potemkin* bears this out. It is amazing how real and sincere its peasants and citizens and seamen are. It is this reality and sincerity that registers so dramatically. No grimaces, no self-conscious gestures, no parboiled theatricals, no glare of studio lights. In *Potemkin* one takes off the godless layer of studio cosmetics and sees through to the living entity.
>
> John Grierson, New York Herald Tribune, 5 December 1926
> in Marshall ed., 1978, p. 229

The review highlights Grierson's prejudices about Eisenstein. His work in British documentary was to exemplify a powerfully selective use of Eisenstein's practice, typage, montage and naturalism. One of its high points is a film like Humphrey Jennings's *Listen to Britain*, but what is interesting is both the ideological gulf between this film and Eisenstein's work; and the way that Jennings offers a seamless associational documentary, more akin to Hollywood's dramatic narratives than the Soviet model.

In post-Second World War cinema *Potemkin* continued to be influential. Neo-realism was indebted to Eisenstein for its realist approach, editing and his particular inflection of protest melodramas. This was the period that developed an international art cinema market, with specialist distributors and cinemas and tied in to a circuit of festivals. The 1960s saw a variety of 'new waves' in Europe and abroad, often strongly influenced by Eisenstein and his contemporaries. The richest area was what has been called Third Cinema. Young film-makers in the countries involved in liberation struggles from Western Imperialism found Eisenstein's political content and expressive style apt for their own, similar circumstances.

Thus, Gillo Pontecorvo's commissioned *The Battle of Algiers*, a seminal text for Third Cinema, shows a range of influences from Eisenstein: its grainy naturalism, powerful sequences of editing, and typage-style casting. A few years later, Jorge Sanjines, in *Blood of the Condor*, again recycled and developed the major styles of Eisenstein's work. The final frame of upraised hands and rifles, referencing both the sailors on *Potemkin* and the crowds on the quay, achieved iconic status in the New Latin American Cinema. The cinema of liberated Cuba would be another example of the influence.

Nearer today, another notable exponent of montage is the Senegalese director, Osmane Sembene. In his 1989 film, *Camp D'Thiaroye*, a massacre by French colonialists echoes Eisenstein's Odessa Steps sequence. At the same time, the film's use of symbolism and motifs, as with the German helmet worn by a concentration camp survivor; or an undelivered packet of coffee for a victim of the massacre, can be seen to continue the filmic rhetoric developed by Eisenstein.

In mainstream contemporary cinema the obvious imitator of Eisenstein would be Oliver Stone's *JFK*, especially in its opening ten minutes, which is in the direct tradition of cinematic montage, whilst his more recent *Natural Born Killers* uses digital imaging to play with montage-style effects. Of course, mainstream cinema is full of pastiche for the modern knowing audience. So the legacy of the Odessa Steps will be most familiar from the variation in Brian De Palma's *The Untouchables*. What is

the joke with the pram

interesting about his homage to *Potemkin* in this film, is that the sequence is so totally Hollywood. Continuity is built and maintained through the star gaze of Kevin Costner, as we cross the multiple lines of the set-up, he always provides a firm anchor. And the joke with the pram is also the total reversal of the pathos of the original.

critical responses

The influence of *Potemkin* has also been exerted by Eisenstein's contribution to cinematic theory. In the 1930s he regularly taught at the Soviet Film schools. He also wrote extensively, though much of this writing has only been published long after his death. It is clear that *Potemkin* represents only a stage in his development. However, its immense success and influence meant that it was an example to which he constantly returned. Since the 1930s also saw the imposition of socialist realism and the crack-down on formalism, those aspects of his theories that apply to montage in terms of editing are most clearly represented by the silent films.

For a period Eisenstein's emphasis on montage as the key to cinematic language held sway for all sorts of theorists. In the 1950s, however, André Bazin counterposed his emphasis on mise-en-scène. He gave preference to directors using deep focus and long takes over the cutting school of Eisenstein. In part this was a reaction against Eisenstein's overemphatic statements on montage. But it also distorted the practice represented by his films. Eisenstein's theories, including montage, ranged beyond editing, so that his films also enjoy a rich mise-en-scène, and also use deep focus, deep staging, and the long take. Moreover, Eisenstein usually avoids claims about montage as the 'essence' of cinema, sharing a total view of art with many of his Soviet contemporaries. And Bazin's strictures for mise-en-scène against editing are not strictly observed in the films he honours. Indeed, one of the great exponents of deep focus, Orson Welles, also relies heavily on montage editing in his films, witness *Citizen Kane* and the breakfast scene, or the inter-cutting in *Touch of Evil*. Bazin's propositions led to a tendency of either/or for a period.

One major critique of Eisenstein and *Potemkin* is in *Film as Film* by

'on screen a granite lion jumped up swiftly'

V.F. Perkins. He focuses on the marble lions, which end the Odessa Steps sequence.

> it seems a serious criticism of Eisenstein's device that the lions served no purpose in the movie beyond that of becoming components of a montage effect. They were not represented as, for example, elements of the Odessa setting, nor as targets for the Potemkin's attack. The absence of connection, in terms of story, action, location – the absence of any dramatic connection at all – entailed an extreme imprecision of effect.
>
> Perkins, 1972, pp. 103–4

Herbert Marshall takes Perkins to task, spending several pages demonstrating how, in fact, the lions can be related to the setting of Odessa. But an equally important point is that Perkins is not judging the lions by the criteria of montage in Eisenstein's sense. The example from *Potemkin* is followed by an example from *Psycho*, the shower sequence, which Perkins praises. But what he likes about *Psycho*, and Hitchcock generally, is how editing techniques both work within and expand Hollywood structures. Eisenstein's montage – and *Potemkin* – offers a different structure. And whilst Hitchcock uses shocks, these are not what Eisenstein means by 'attractions'. Pudovkin comments on the same lions:

> The three different lions (sleeping, rising, standing) were joined together in such a way that on screen a granite lion jumped up swiftly. These unusual jumps of bronze and stone, suddenly interrupting the flight of clouds of smoke and the collapse of stone columns, were so stunningly unexpected in their emotional effect, they matched so perfectly the shots of the explosion, that the effect on the audience was one of unprecedented force. The explosion on the screen was literally deafening. The audience applauded not because it was pleased but because it was shaken.
>
> *From Potemkin to October, 1928*
> in Taylor & Christie eds, 1993, p. 199

More recent critical engagements with Eisenstein and his famous film have been less concerned to draw lines of demarcation. They generally display a sympathy for his approach, whilst critically deconstructing it.

critical responses contexts

a stark conflict between evil and innocence

One line is the question of *Potemkin*'s reconstruction of recorded history (K.R.M. Short ed., 1981). D.J. Wenden examines some of the discrepancies between the history of the *Potemkin* mutiny and the filmic version. He notes some of the inaccuracies, major and minor. The two *causes célèbres* are the tarpaulin thrown over the mutineers in Part II, and the Odessa Steps in Part IV. In fact, whilst Wenden notes Eisenstein's claim that he invented the tarpaulin incident, a naval history (Hough, 1960) thinks it was, in fact, a not uncommon occurrence. With the Odessa Steps, Eisenstein has effectively transformed a muddled mix of demonstrations, criminality and repression into a stark conflict between evil and innocence. This volume, by siting the discussion of *Potemkin* alongside analyses of films like *The Way Ahead* or *Casablanca*, avoids the stereotyping of propaganda films found in conservative critics.

More contemporary discussion has been concerned with Eisenstein's relationship to sexual politics and to the concerns of semiology, i.e. film as a system of communications analysable as signs. A key text here is Andrew Britton's two-part article for *Framework* (1977–8). This concentrates on *October*, and to a lesser degree on *Ivan the Terrible*. However, it does include some comment on *Potemkin*: '*Potemkin* celebrates the revolution as an emanation of male vitality which makes possible the joyful expression of male unity and comradeship' (Andrew Britton, 1977, p. 9). He continues, examining the problematic representation of women in *October* in particular. Developing this critique Nestor Almendros (1991) has related images in *Potemkin* to Eisenstein as gay. He particularly discusses the images in Part I of the film with the images of the semi-naked sailors in their hammocks. He also notes how these striking images are not matched when we see the inhabitants of Odessa. He comments on the difference between the representation of men and of women in the film.

This is a major point in a discussion by Judith Mayne (1982). *Potemkin* is one example for Mayne of the problem of gender in Soviet Montage films. She points to the limitations of women's politics in the Bolshevik revolution. It worth noting that initially the new Soviet society created progressive change for all sorts of groups; specifically both homosexuals and women benefited from the abolition of reactionary laws. However,

THE BATTLESHIP POTEMKIN

both groups were to lose such new-found freedoms in the more conservative era of the 1930s. Mayne argues that the problem goes beyond the parameters of contemporary culture and politics; she argues that montage, and the montage in *Potemkin* in particular, is structured to the detriment of women characters. She goes on to claim:

> However, despite Eisenstein's claims that Potemkin was structured as an 'organic whole' and as a five-part tragedy, the relationship between this famous sequence and other parts of the film, particularly the conclusion, is unclear, and less 'organic' than Eisenstein claims. The confusion stems, to a large extent, from the ambiguous function of female figures in the film and, in particular, from the relationship between those figures and the masses which the film ostensibly celebrates.
>
> Mayne, 1982, pp. 30–1

Her argument develops in a complex manner, and a little later she adds, 'my point is that sexual opposition informs the tension between the concrete and the abstract. a tension which is central to the textual workings of the film' (Judith Mayne, 1982, p. 35). She illustrates this by focusing on the pince-nez, of both the doctor and the female victim on the steps, and claiming that both are the object of a metaphor for blindness. In this sense the celebratory thrust of the film, an example of montage, is restricted to the male sailors.

Mayne's article raises some stimulating questions. However, I would argue that her argument fails to nail the problem to montage. In her essay she discusses examples of montage both by Eisenstein and Dovzhenko; unfortunately, the differences between their understandings of this concept parallel differences in political line amongst the Bolsheviks – Soviet cinema is about montages. Equally her detailed textual analysis of *Potemkin* does not quite match the film. She claims at one point that the Odessa Steps sequence features a 'pre-dominance of female bodies', and 'women victims ... appear to be mothers with children'. My counter point is that the steps feature predominantly victims, women and children, and older men, and crippled men: the distinctions go beyond gender. Also, in the steps feature predominantly victims, women and children ...

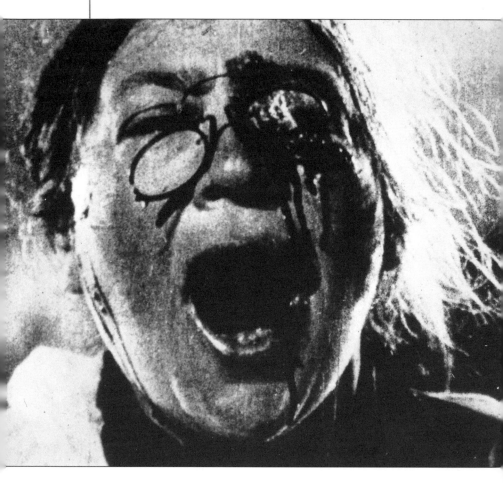

Literal and
rhetorical blindness

fact, the film and the steps feature a range of women, some abstracted, notably the woman in the jump cuts who is unknown. Then Mayne builds an analogy on the abstraction of the stone lions and the idealised male seamen in the final part, however, this leaves aside Eisenstein's deliberate use of caesuras, which presumably means that the spectator is unlikely to go from one idealised image straight to the other. The representation of males in *Potemkin* relies not only on montage, but flows from the heroicisation within the narrative. This is a general tendency in Soviet film of the period. Thus a major problem in *Potemkin* is that the events depicted are supposed to represent the whole of 1905. Yet major groups involved in that revolution are subordinated. Thus, crucially, the sailing away from Odessa after the massacre on the Steps excludes the cross-class and cross-gender alliances which continued to fight against autocracy. What is presented to the audience is male bonding on the open sea, an open space devoid of the social structures found on shore.

All three writers raise serious critical questions about the film and Eisenstein's work more generally. That the whole Soviet montage school endures a gender problem can be seen by one instance – only one major woman director, Esfir Shub, and she is the mistress of that least discussed film form, the compilation documentary.

One other important article by D.L. Selden discusses the 'Rhetoric of Potemkin' (D.L. Selden, 1982). He notes how Eisenstein posits an active spectator, 'reading' the text closely. The film would offer not just meaning through formal structure and style, but through 'imagistic rhetoric', where 'the image was to become 'supra-representational' (ibid., p. 310). He discusses (again) the pince-nez of Doctor Smirnov (see Style). He also discusses the plate-smashing scene in Part I. He notes how the intertitles fragment the quotation of the plate:

> 'GIVE US THIS DAY OUR ...' [title followed by shot, then,]
>
> 'THIS DAY OUR DAILY BR ...' [title followed by shot,]
>
> 'Y OUR DAILY BREAD, GI...'
>
> Mayer, 1962, pp. 64–5

Selden comments: 'To heighten the tension, Eisenstein reassembles the action abstractly as a collage of fragments which seem to rain down upon the eyes of the viewer' (D.L. Selden, 1982, p. 312). Again this fragmentation builds into a motif, with the fragmentation of discipline, the unity of the ship, and eventually, the apparent calm of the city of Odessa. This sort of analysis offers a rich trawl through the extremely detailed and complex meaning inscribed in the film. It is difficult analysis, partly because it carries a heavy load of terminology. The very exact use of language does enable a commentary to distinguish the range of techniques Eisenstein uses to affect the viewer.

conclusion

There is no doubt that Sergei Eisenstein and his most famous film, *Potemkin*, enjoy canonic status in film studies. Not only do the films continue to circulate, but there is a thriving publishing industry on this great auteur. *Potemkin* comes early in the Eisenstein *oeuvre*, and after this film both his theories and practices developed decisively. A later film like *October* is key to his theories about cinematic form. His last work, *Ivan the Terrible*, is a masterwork that, at least formally, completes his canon. What would seem to distinguish *Potemkin* is that it marks the most expressive moment in his career, and indeed, in Soviet montage. There is a convergence in this film of the political, the ideological and the aesthetic. At a moment when Soviet cinema managed to produce the production resources, the ideological climate gave space for invention and expression, and the revolutionary artistic milieu had developed a degree of clarity in its theory and praxis. Eisenstein and *Potemkin* are the supreme achievement of Soviet montage, itself the cutting edge of Soviet revolutionary culture. However, the moment, at least as much as the man, is responsible for this.

bibliography

general

Altman, Rick, *Film Genre*,
Routledge, 1981
  Detailed exploration of film genres

Bordwell, David, *Narration in the Fiction Film*, Routledge, 1985
  A detailed study of narrative theory and structures

– – – *The Classical Hollywood Cinema: Film Style & Mode of Production to 1960*, Routledge, 1985; pprbk 1995
  An authoritative study of cinema as institution, it covers film style and production

Bordwell, David & Thompson, Kristin, *Film Art*, McGraw-Hill, 4th edn, 1993
  An introduction to film aesthetics for the non-specialist

Branson, Gill & Stafford, Roy, *The Media Studies Handbook*,
Routledge, 1996

Buckland, Warren, *Teach Yourself Film Studies*, Hodder & Stoughton, 1998
  Very accessible, it gives an overview of key areas in film studies

Cook, Pam (ed.), *The Cinema Book*,
British Film Institute, 1994

Corrigan, Tim,
A Short Guide To Writing About Film,
HarperCollins, 1994
  What it says: a practical guide for students

Dyer, Richard, *Stars*, London BFI, 1979
  A good introduction to the star system

Easthope, Antony, *Classical Film Theory*, Longman, 1993
  A clear overview of recent writing about film theory

Hayward, Susan, *Key Concepts in Cinema Studies*, Routledge, 1996

Hill, & Gibson (eds), *The Oxford Guide to Film Studies*, Oxford, 1998
  Wide-ranging standard guide

Lapsley, Robert & Westlake, Michael, *Film Theory: An Introduction*,
Manchester University Press, 1994

Maltby, Richard & Craven, Ian, *Hollywood Cinema*,
Blackwell, 1995
  A comprehensive work on the Hollywood industry and its products

Nelmes, Jill (ed.),
Introduction to Film Studies,
Routledge, 1996
  Deals with several national cinemas and key concepts in film study

Nowell-Smith, Geoffrey (ed.),
The Oxford History of World Cinema,
Oxford, 1996
  Hugely detailed and wide-ranging with many features on 'stars'

Thomson, David, *A Biographical Dictionary of the Cinema*,
Secker & Warburg, 1975
  Unashamedly driven by personal taste, but often stimulating

Truffaut, François, *Hitchcock*,
New York, Simon & Schuster, 1966, rev.ed. Touchstone, 1985
  Landmark extended interview

Turner, Graham, *Film as Social Practice*,
Routledge, 1993

Wollen, Peter,
Signs and Meaning in the Cinema,
New York, Viking 1972
  An important study in semiology

battleship potemkin   bibliography

Readers should also explore the many relevant websites and journals. *Film Education* and *Sight and Sound* are standard reading.

Valuable websites include:

The Internet Movie Database at
http://uk.imdb.com/

Screensite at
http://www.tcf.ua.edu/screensite/contents.htm

The Media and Communications Site at the University of Aberystwyth at
http://www.aber.ac.uk/~dgc/welcome.html

There are obviously many other university and studio websites which are worth exploring in relation to film studies.

the battleship potemkin

Almendros, Nestor, 'Fortune and Men's Eyes', *Film Comment*, vol.27, no.4, Jul/Aug, 1991
> A discussion of *Potemkin*, including its gay aspects

Bergan, Ronald, *Eisenstein, A Life in Conflict*, Little Brown & Co. 1997
> The most recent biography, making good use of newly available source material

Bordwell, David, *The Cinema of Eisenstein*, Harvard University Press, 1993
> A key commentary on Eisenstein, his milieu and the films

Britton, Andrew, 'Sexuality and Power', *Framework*, no.6, 1977 and no.7/8, 1978
> A key article, in two parts, focusing on *October* and *Ivan the Terrible*

Christie, Ian & Taylor, Richard, eds, *Eisenstein Rediscovered*, Routledge, 1993
> Some of the most recent critical articles on Eisenstein, including a helpful introduction by Ian Christie, and *Eisenstein's Early Films Abroad* by Kristin Thompson

Eisenstein, Sergei, *Film Form Essays in Film Theory*, ed. and trans. Jay Leyda, Denis Dobson Ltd, London, 1951
> An early collection of some of Eisenstein's writings on film and film theory

Buñuel, Luis, trans. by Abigail Israel, *My Last Breath – The Autobiography*, Jonathan Cape, 1984
> His life and films, witty and absorbing

Eisenstein, Sergei, *The Battleship Potemkin*, trans. Gillon R. Aitken, Lorrimer Publishing Ltd, 1968
> The published script. Produced after the film was finished, presumably from shooting scripts, etc.

Hough, Richard, *The Potemkin Mutiny*, Prentice-Hall, Inc., 1960
> A naval history of the famous mutiny

Kuleshov, Lev, trans. and ed., Ronald Levaco, *Kuleshov on Film, Writings of Lev Kuleshov*, University of California Press, 1974
> The writings of a key pioneer in Soviet film and montage

Leyda, Jay, ed., *Three Films*, Lorrimer Publishing Ltd, 1974
Contains the shooting script by Eisenstein and an extract from the original script by Eisenstein and Agadzhanova-Shutko

Leyda, Jay, *Kino, A History of the Russian and Soviet Film*, George Allen & Unwin Ltd, 1960
An essential source, even though newer works have been published

Marshall, Herbert, ed., *The Battleship Potemkin*, Avon, 1978
A compilation of material by the film-makers, contemporaries and subsequent critics. A great source book, copies held in the British Library and the BFI Library

Mayer, David, *Eisenstein's Potemkin, A Shot-by-Shot Presentation*, Da Capo Paperback, 1972
An impressive aid to close analysis

Mayne, Judith, 'Soviet Film Montage and the Woman Question', *Camera Obscura*, no.19, January 1989
This study focuses on the montage films of Eisenstein and Dovzhenko

Montagu, Ivor, *With Eisenstein in Hollywood*, Seven Seas Books, 1968
Montagu's recollections of Eisenstein's tour of Europe and, especially, the USA

Perkins, Victor, F., *Film as Film*, Penguin Books, 1972
A now classic text on film theory and analysis

Selden, D.L., 'The Rhetoric of Potemkin', *Quarterly Review of Film Studies*, vol.7, no.4, Fall 1982
A discussion of rhetorical devices in the films of Eisenstein

Seton, Marie, *Sergei M. Eisenstein*, Grove Press, Inc. New York, 1960
First full-scale biography, eminently readable and full of important data

Short, K.R.M., ed., *Feature Films as History*, Croom Helm, 1981
A number of articles which discuss how fictional films handle the record of our past

Sudendorf, Werner, 'Revolte im Orchestergraben Zur Biographie Edmund Meisels', *Kinematograph*, no.i, 1984. Trans. and summary Julia Shemilt, 1999
There is a copy of the article in the BFI Reading Room

Taylor, Richard, ed. and trans., *Eisenstein, Selected Works, Volume 1, Writings, 1922–34*, BFI Publishing, 1988
New translations and excellent supporting scholarship. Four volumes in all – all impressively stimulating

Taylor, Richard, ed., trans. William Powell, *Beyond the Stars: The Memoirs of Sergei Eisenstein*, BFI Publishing, 1995
A warts-and-all self-portrait: you get a sense of his quirky humour and dazzling erudition

Taylor, Richard & Christie, Ian, eds, *The Film Factory*, Routledge, 1988
Important documents from Russian and Soviet Cinema. A companion volume, also edited by Richard Taylor & Ian Christie, *Inside the Film Factory*, Routledge, 1991, has articles on both Russian and Soviet Cinema

Walker Michael, 'Melodrama and the American Cinema', *Movie*, no. 29/30, 1982
  Contains the shooting script by Eisenstein and an extract from the original script by Eisenstein and Agadzhanova-Shutko

Weinberg, Robert, *The Revolution of 1905 in Odessa*, Indiana University Press, 1993
  A detailed study of the whole year of revolution in the city

Withall, Keith, *Eisenstein Study Pack*, 1999, *In The Picture* Publications, West Yorkshire
  Designed for teachers and students

Tsivian, Yuri, 'Between the Old and the New: Soviet Film Culture in 1918–1924', *Griffithiana*, no.55/56, September 1996
  A study of the transition between pre- and post-revolutionary cinema

filmography

Currently, versions of *The Battleship Potemkin* available are:

■ The Film Society print from 1929, intertitles translated by Ivor Montagu
Uncensored as it was not for public screenings (available from the BFI)

■ The Museum of Modern Art print
Relatively complete (silent print from Contemporary and BFI); run at silent
speeds with the Meisel score (found on the Tartan Video and Russian
Classics Video)

■ The Kryukov accompanied version
Step-printed for sound and suffering from censors' cuts (Contemporary
and BFI, also on The Russian Classics Video)

■ The Shostakovich accompanied version
Again step-printed, but relatively complete (available from Contemporary
and the BFI, available on DVD on the Internet)

■ Libra Productions
A version using material from the 1970s' stretched print, but used without
a sound track and often accompanied by live performances of the Meisel
score (held by the BFI)

■ The Munich Restoration (by Eno Patalas)
A silent print, and the longest, 1,740 metres (held at the Munich Film
Archive, screened once at the NFT in 1998)

cinematic terms

aspect ratio   the relationship between the horizontal and vertical dimensions of the screen shape, the shape and expression varied between 1.17:1 and 1.33:1 for early cinema; modern cinema varies between 1.60:1 and 1.85:1, with cinemascope reaching 2.4:1

auteurisme   the emphasis on one key person, usually the director, as the source of style and meaning in a film. The French term stems from the impact of auteuriste arguments about Hollywood directors, such as Hitchcock, Wyler, Ray and others, by the French critics of the 1950s

closure   the resolution of the narrative by an ending which both satisfies the viewer, often therefore 'happy', and also resolves the different threads of the narrative, e.g. marries lovers, solves murders, punishes villains and so on

diegesis   the world of the story. So all the events on board and in Odessa are part of the diegesis, whereas the lions would seem to be non-diegetic, from outside the story world

ellipsis   the cutting out of time, hence shortening or compressing the time span. There does not seem to be a set word for expanding time, as with the use of overlapping montage: expansion probably serves

formalism   in the world of Soviet art this was an epithet. Artists and artworks displaying formalism were deemed to be failing in addressing the masses. So experimentation, unusual or difficult narrative and stylistic effects, modernist devices, were all deemed to be unsuitable for the agitational role assigned to art. Eisenstein, especially, fell foul of these strictures. Godard's later epithet about the 'Hollywood-Mosfilm axis' is an apt

comment on how Soviet film became as conventionalised as its Hollywood opposite

fps   the speed at which the film passes in front of the lens of either camera or projector. Early film speeds ran as slow as 14fps – sound standardised the speed at 24fps

intertitle   a title card that conveys plot, dialogue and comment or interpretation in silent films

jump cut   a cut between two shots that appears abrupt and therefore noticeable. Changes of camera positions are usually at least 30% to avoid this. Cuts are often made on movement or sound cues to cover the change

long take   a shot that runs longer than the norm

Marxism & class   not of course a film term but one necessary in understanding *Potemkin*. Put very simply, proletarians sell their labour power (their ability to make things) to capitalists (bourgeoisie), who, because they own the means of production (factories, machines, patents, etc.) can both employ the workers and make profits from the value produced when workers turn objects of use into objects that can be sold. Bargaining for a larger slice of the profits does not resolve the fundamental exploitation, hence Communists (like the Bolsheviks) advocate seizing the means of production. Seizing State Power is considered necessary to effect and safeguard control. Caught between proletarians and capitalists are the petty bourgeoisie (not quite the English 'middle classes'). They are distinguished by either not having to sell their labour power directly, or not selling it for production. But neither do they own capital. If not always easy to identify exactly, their tendency to vacillate between the two major classes is commonly apparent. In *Potemkin*, the sailors share a proletarian status with the workers of Odessa. Because of the events of 1905, many of the middling strata – shop-keepers, teachers, intellectuals – take common ground with them. But the bourgeoisie proper, as with the land-owning and officer classes, are clearly with the exploiters. The Tsar is running a state that protects their interests

metonymy substituting a word closely associated with an object for the object itself: a rhetorical term used in some film analysis

mise-en-scène French, meaning staging. So, everything that goes in front of the camera, the visual composition, usually broken down into sets or locations; lighting; acting and movement; props and costumes

montage for Eisenstein this covers the whole range of techniques that produce both the clash of ideas and the stimulation of new ideas in the viewer. More specifically in Soviet Cinema it refers to the use of fast editing to shock and/or stimulate the viewer through the collision of images, a function of editing. It is used in a more general sense to refer to fast editing, often in a short sequence, as when time is shown rapidly passing.

overtonal montage Eisenstein's concept that describes not only changes between shots, but variations within shots. He quotes as an example the changing tones of the harbour in morning mist in

Potemkin. overlapping montage a cut where the succeeding shot does not just continue the action or image of the preceding one, but actually repeats a section, a number of frames. Thus, on the Odessa Steps, we actually see the mother and child traverse the same steps twice, in different shots

narrative what we call stories. A series of events, organised in time and space, usually causally related. In narrative we distinguish between story: everything that happens, including parts filled in by the audience; and plot: what is actually presented to the audience. In *Potemkin*, the audience will presumably fill in other events from 1905 not actually in the plotting

semiology the study of texts, including films, as a system of communications. A film is conceived as a vast map of signs (the red flag signs both the mutinous ship and the revolutionary spirit) which the audience reads, but which the analyst can also tabulate and discuss

step-printing adding frames to a film so that it can run at sound speed without the jerky movement caused by increasing the frames per second. It is usual to add an extra frame for every two in the original print. It works up to a point for films shot at 16fps, but is obviously a problem for films shot at 20+fps. It is also a problem when the editing works with very short and exact shots, as in sections of *Potemkin*

synecdoche the part standing in for the whole: a rhetorical term used in some film analysis

credits

production company
First Goskino Productions, Moscow

director
Sergei Eisenstein

producer
Jacob Bliokh

scenario and script
Sergei Eisenstein

original story
Nina Agadzhanova-Shutko in collaboration with Sergei Eisenstein

photography
Eduard Tissé

art director
Vasili Rakhals

assistant director
Grigory Alexandrov

assistants to Eisenstein
A. Antonov, A. Levshin, M. Gomorov, M. Shtrauk, L. Kryukov

camera assistant
V. Popov

subtitles
Nikolai Asseyev (poet born in 1889)

length
1,640 metres

shot during
July–November 1925

locations
Leningrad, at Odessa and aboard the *Twelve Apostles* (the sister ship of the *Prince Potemkin of Taurida*) which was aground in the Bay of Sevastopol

edited
November–December 1925 in Moscow

cast
Vakulinchuk – A. Antonov
Commander Golikov – Vladimir Barsky
Senior Officer Gilyarovsky – Grigory Alexandrov
Sailor Matyushenko – M. Gomorov
Ship's Surgeon Smirnov – An anonymous workman
Priest – An anonymous old gardener from the orchards on the outskirts of Sevastopol
Boatswain – Levchenko
Woman on the steps – Repnikova
Officer – Marusov
Others –
Sailors of the Red Navy
Citizens of Odessa
Members of the Proletcult Theatre

Other titles in the series

Other titles available in the York Film Notes series:

Title	ISBN
8½	0582 40488 6
A Bout de Souffle	0582 43182 4
Apocalypse Now	0582 43183 2
Battleship Potemkin	0582 40490 8
Blade Runner	0582 43198 0
Casablanca	0582 43201 4
Chinatown	0582 43199 9
Citizen Kane	0582 40493 2
Das Cabinet des Dr Caligari	0582 40494 0
Double Indemnity	0582 43196 4
Dracula	0582 43197 2
Easy Rider	0582 43195 6
Fargo	0582 43193 X
La Haine	0582 43194 8
Lawrence of Arabia	0582 43192 1
Psycho	0582 43191 3
Pulp Fiction	0582 40510 6
Romeo and Juliet	0582 43189 1
Some Like It Hot	0582 40503 3
Stagecoach	0582 43187 5
Taxi Driver	0582 40506 8
Terminator	0582 43186 7
The Full Monty	0582 43181 6
The Godfather	0582 43188 3
The Piano	0582 43190 5
The Searchers	0582 40510 6
The Third Man	0582 40511 4
Thelma and Louise	0582 43184 0
Unforgiven	0582 43185 9

Also from York Notes

Also available in the **York Notes** range:

York Notes
The ultimate literature guides for GCSE students (or equivalent levels)

York Notes Advanced
Literature guides for A-level and undergraduate students (or equivalent levels)

York Personal Tutors
Personal Tutoring on essential GCSE English and Maths topics

Available from good bookshops.
For full details, please visit our website at www.longman-yorknotes.com